I'm Tough . . .
And I Cry a Lot

Jaimie Sherling

ISBN: 979-8-36-818132-5

Library of Congress Control #2022923282

Contents

This is dedicated to everyone
who has loved and supported me
And the people who kept asking about a second book.

LOVE

———————————

EVERYTHING

A LITTLE MORE

And...I realized I still have a bit more to say.

What possessed me to write another book? To be fair, one could ask the same question about my first go-round. So, let's take a little trip down memory lane.

In the spring of 2020, I had too much time on my hands. *Same old. Same old.* I still worked from home. Which was fine. And minus a quick venture out for groceries, I stayed home. All. The. Time. Not so fine.

Completely alone with my thoughts, I wrote the bulk of my first book. More than idle hands and frustration with the world, I had something to say. I needed to tell everyone how much the FIVE community meant to me. I needed to share the journey I'd been through. How I'd driven to FIVE Nightclub countless evenings to cheer on fabulous drag queens even when I'd looked sick. And in all fairness, I had been doing weekly chemotherapy at the time. Breast cancer had taken away my breasts and my hair. Because of the seriousness of my diagnosis and genetic testing, my surgeon had recommended a double mastectomy. For many personal reasons, I chose not to have reconstructive surgery. But at FIVE, while at my lowest, the queens had lifted me up and become dear friends. When I'd finally finished the edits on that book, I told myself never again. I said the same to anyone who asked. Nope. Nope. Nope. And nope.

"You never know. Maybe write some notes, just in case," my friend Adam argued. We'd met at FIVE during summer volleyball in 2019. In a year full of drag shows and random trips to Culver's, the pediatric resident had become my soulmate. The best version of a platonic soulmate.

Adam did not relent. My first book released, and he messaged me the next day.

Adam: OMG!! I got notified that my book shipped tonight.

Me: <Three heart eye emojis>

Adam: I've been telling you for weeks. You need to start on volume two.

Me: Yeah yeah yeah

Five days later, I hiked to my favorite spot overlooking Lake Mendota with my notebook and shot him a message.

Me: You win. I came to write a little.

Did I listen to everything Adam said? No. Well, mostly no. He was right a few times though. When he gave advice, especially when he was serious about it, I at least tried to hear him out. So, why would I write another book? Because people like my friend Kay said, "But you have to keep writing."

But did I, Kay? Was I so used to the grind that I didn't know how to have down time? Maybe? Should I write because it was the closest thing to talking nonstop? Could be. My sixth, seventh, and eighth grade teachers had all told me I talked too much. They were right.

Chapter One

NOW WHAT?

G ROWING UP WITH SEVEN siblings, I learned early to be careful with money. My dad worked hard to pay the bills. My mom worked hard at home raising us. I expected the same work ethic for myself. I planned my future—get good grades, go to college, find a job that allowed me to take care of myself.

After I graduated from college, I started teaching kindergarten. A good plan that seemed to be working. Until August 2019 when my husband moved out, and I couldn't pay my mortgage. Ashamed, I beat myself up for the choices I'd made that had led me where I was. I wasn't too proud to admit that I attended more than one pity party for myself. At the end of the day though, my kids needed someplace to stay when it was my week to have them. So, I got creative and rented out the basement room. I made great memories and decent money. For that month. But it wasn't sustainable. I needed a regular income. Since I lived a few miles from the university, I decided to post a room for rent on sites for students.

In a matter of days, Katherine texted me.

Katherine: Hello Jamie, I saw your property listed, and I'm extremely interested in the space and would like to know more about it if it's still available. Thank you for your time. Looking forward to hearing back from you soon.

Point deducted for misspelling my name. Point added back for being super professional. Yep, I could work with that.

Katherine and I met in person, and I knew we'd be a fit the second she said, "I'm the oldest of four and have a brother your kids' age." She mostly kept to herself, but we all got along. She became a regular at my monthly brunch. And I had a viable solution.

Until March 2020 when the university announced all classes would be online for the rest of the semester. Thank you, COVID.

Katherine kept working at the coffee shop, and I worked from home. Two weeks later, I noticed her room was very tidy as I passed by to change the laundry. Huh. That was odd. Katherine usually lived in a pigsty. But she paid rent on time, and I could live with a mess I rarely saw.

The next morning, she broke the news. "They're closing the dorms. I need to drive my sister back to Virginia."

That made sense with everything being virtual.

"I'm not sure if I'm coming back," she added.

"Okay," I said, because I had no idea what else to say. But it was so not okay.

"Since I don't have a full-time job here, I might not be able to get back into the state."

COVID, the gift that kept on giving.

"But I set money aside so I can pay you for the next two months," she offered.

"Oh, that would be great." Phew. At least I had a cushion now.

I felt bad accepting her money if she wasn't going to be living with me. But the bank wasn't about to feel bad for me, and she *had* signed my weak version of a lease.

Three days later, the house was so quiet, and I wanted to know that she'd gotten home safely, so I texted her.

I got crickets.

That was okay. We weren't besties. Or related. Or in a relationship.

Two weeks later, I texted again.

Nothing. She ghosted me, and I never heard from her again.

Panicked, I started going through my options. Could I find a new renter during a global pandemic? Good luck with that. A stimulus check saved me for two months. But what then? I was grateful to still have my job, that it was already remote, but it wasn't enough to pay my bills. Maybe I could refinance and lower my monthly payment?

I emailed the mortgage loan officer, completed the paperwork, and emailed bank statements. I scheduled a time for the appraiser to visit. Only to have my hopes dashed. The appraisal number was too low. I could only refinance with a co-borrower. That was a hard pass. I sat at my computer and cried. A lot.

The next day I went back into solution mode and reached out to my realtor friend Nicole.

Me: Hi! I have real estate questions for you when you're available.

Nicole: Sure, what's up?

Me: I know you said it's a good time to sell because inventory is low. Are sellers getting good offers (God forbid bidding wars/multiple offers) like a few years ago?

Nicole: Yes! It's cray right now. And they're all starting to come out of the woodwork. If you want to do it, I'd tell you to do it NOW.

Two days later, my house went on the market and a "For Sale" sign landed in my front lawn ninja-style.

That afternoon, I texted Jess. I needed to process with a friend who wasn't my realtor.

Me: Soooo I'm putting my house on the market.

Jess: Really?!?? How come?

Me: Honestly, Glennon Doyle was part of it. <shocked face emoji>

Side note: Jess had told me repeatedly that I needed to read Glennon Doyle's third book, *Untamed*. I'd listened, bought it, and devoured it.

Me: I was trying to refinance to have the house in my name only (and be more affordable). Late on Wednesday night, I found out my appraisal wasn't high enough. Then I read this from *Untamed*. "What is better: uncomfortable truth or comfortable lies?"

Jess: Oof. That's a lot to take in.

At the end of the day, being in my house was a comfortable lie. The truth was, I couldn't afford it. At all.

Chapter Two

EXTROVERT

I OWNED A CHARMING house in a desirable neighborhood in Madison. As soon as the listing went live, my phone blew up with showing requests. When I'd put my last house on the market, I'd happily left during showings, rotating between the library and a coffee shop. Neither was an option with COVID. At least the weather was warm. I drove down to the lake and meandered until it was safe to return.

On May 27, a potential buyer requested an evening showing. Okay, fine. I decided to order myself dinner and make my own picnic. Late in the afternoon, I called the Otter Tavern. "Hi! Can I place an order for pickup?"

"Sure can," the host responded. "The patio's open too."

"It is?" I didn't think any restaurants were open for in-person dining.

"Yes, today's our first day back," he explained.

"I'll stop by tonight. Thanks so much."

Just as I sent my last work email for the day, Adam texted me.

Adam: Want to get a drink???

Me: That sounds great!!! I was gonna treat myself to Otter Tavern tonight.

Adam: I'm getting dinner with Rachel.

Adam had met Rachel through his residency program, and I'd met her when we were both backup dancers for Adam's drag persona, Electra Lytes. They had a lot to celebrate, just weeks away from finishing their residency programs. Adam already had a job waiting for him in September in La Crosse.

Me: NICE!!

Adam: You'd be more than welcome to join us, or I could meet you somewhere after.

Me: I'd love to see her, but she might appreciate the time for just the two of you.

Adam: Okay, I'll call when we're done.

Me: Okay. Can't wait to see you!

Adam: Where do you want to go?

Me: I don't know. Did you have an idea? We could always sit on my patio and drink. <shrug emoji> <crying laughing emoji>

We left our plans there, and I slipped on my sandals. Just around the corner, I arrived at the tavern five minutes later. I grinned when I saw the familiar metal patio tables and chairs back on the cement alongside the sidewalk. It had been far too long. I ordered my regular burger and fries. Knowing I'd be drinking with

Adam before too long, I drank water. The warm spring air felt amazing on my skin. I soaked it up and sent a selfie to my best friend KG, who lived in Austin. I looked around and saw so many smiling faces. It didn't hurt that people were out in public for the first time in over two months.

Then it started to drizzle, and the table next to me scrambled to go inside.

I smiled. "It's fine, it's just sprinkling." And I wasn't stuck in my house. So, yay!

One extra friendly diner grinned back and followed the rest of his table inside.

Bigger raindrops fell, the universe taunting my decision.

I caved, grabbed my plate, and rushed inside. I passed him and sat at the opposite end of the bar.

"Guess it was too much rain after all?" he teased, and tipped his head toward the front door.

"I draw the line at soggy fries."

The rain stopped, and I went back outside. Global pandemic aside, there was something special about sitting on a patio after months of winter weather. I didn't want to rush Adam's dinner with Rachel. I also had no reason to hurry home.

The friendly crew made their way back out to the patio too.

When I was finally ready to go home, I weaved through the surrounding tables to say goodbye.

"Why don't you join us?" the same guy asked.

I thought about it for a second. Why not? We were sitting outside. Distanced. They seemed harmless. And I missed peopling. "Sure." I grabbed a chair.

"I'm Otis," the guy told me.

"I'm Jaimie. Nice to officially meet you." I sat down across from him.

"I'm Dylan." The brunette guy next to Otis introduced himself—and reached out to shake my hand.

No, thank you. We *were* still in a global pandemic. "Hi." I put up my hands in front of me, then awkwardly waved.

"I'm Kinzy," the only female in the group said.

"And I'm Jack," the guy sitting across from me offered.

Okay. Full stop. Clear ocean blue eyes and a warm smile. This one was cute. No complaints here.

We all chatted for a while, then Otis asked, "Want a drink?"

"Sure." I could have one while I waited for Adam. Speaking of, he had a sixth sense, that guy. Or it was a soulmate thing. Minutes later, he texted.

Adam: Hey, Rachel had to drive me home because I drank too much <crying emoji>.

Me: Okayyyyy. So, another time?

Adam: I'm sorry ☹

Me: It's okay. You needed to let loose. Glad Rachel was there for you. I just met some people at Otter Tavern, and I already got a drink.

Adam: Okay perfect!

An hour flew by, and Otis pointed to my empty glass. "Another?"

Why not? I'd be walking home. My extrovert soul soaked up spending time with actual people in real life. While I was grateful for technology, video calls didn't quite cut it.

After another hour, Jack had an idea. "Let's keep the party going."

I was so happy to be social, and we'd been hanging out this long already, so I agreed. They seemed cool. I felt safe with another woman in the group. "I live around the corner. We can hang on my patio."

Otis and Jack drove to get more alcohol while Dylan and Kinzy followed me home.

We sat around my patio table as the sun started to set behind the trees in my backyard.

Otis asked, "So, you're selling your house?"

I guess that big sign in the front yard left little to the imagination. "Yeah, time for a change." They didn't need to know my personal business.

"It looks like a really cute house. I'd like to check it out."

"I think it is," I beamed. I really did love where I lived.

Otis smiled and announced to the table, "I'm friends with Nicole, your realtor."

"No way." I shook my head.

"I am. Call her." He threw his head back a little for added emphasis.

I dialed her number immediately. "Hey, Nicole, I'm here with Otis."

"You're where?" she nearly shrieked into my ear.

I was surprised by the shock in her voice. Otis seemed super friendly. If she knew him at all, I thought she'd expect a night like this from him. "At my house. I met Otis and some of his friends during dinner."

"Really? How did that happen?" she sounded dumbfounded.

"We met at the Otter Tavern and decided to come back here." I still didn't understand why this was a big deal.

"And you're all okay?" Why did she sound so nervous? Why would we not be okay?

"We are. Otis wants to look at the house tomorrow." I smiled. Could it really be this easy to sell a house?

Her tone changed. Ever the professional, she got back to business. "Okay, I'll schedule a showing, and I'll see him tomorrow," she replied.

"Good night," I chirped.

"Good night." She clipped her words, and the call ended before I even pulled the phone away from my ear.

A little while later, my guests took turns going inside to use the bathroom. That made me a little uncomfortable. But I wasn't going to make them go outside. I wasn't a monster. The night was going so well. I gave a quick tour of the house. I mean, I might as well give them my take on it. Otis was going to be back the next day for a showing.

Back outside, we regrouped back at the patio table. We talked and laughed. After something particularly funny, I threw my whole body back cackling, and my hand brushed Jack's leg as I sat forward.

Minutes later, he took a small square of tin foil out of his pocket. He set it on the table and opened it up.

I saw white powder, and my mind raced. I'd only seen cocaine in TV shows and movies. Was this guy about to snort coke on my patio table?

Jack casually looked over at me. "Want some?"

"No, I'm good." Nothing else to say, I checked on Adam.

Me: You okay?

Adam: Yes! Hahaha

Me: Ok. So, four people are drinking on my patio... <grimacing face emoji> <shrug emoji> <crying laughing emoji>

Adam: Awwwww. Who?

I texted one picture of Otis and Dylan sitting across from me and another of Jack.

Adam: Fun!

Me: I'm having so much fun! I have a story for tomorrow!

The table got quiet. It was time to call it a night, and everyone left. I watched their taillights fade as they drove out of my driveway and down the street.

Chapter Three

STORY FOR TOMORROW

T HE NEXT MORNING, I woke up with a headache. Not surprising. I'd drank more alcohol than I should've. A couple ibuprofen, and I'd move on with my day. I walked into the bathroom.

And found my dress on the floor.

That was weird. I never changed in there. I stared at it a moment. Something was definitely off. I sat down to pee. The second I started to go, I screamed. It burned like rubbing alcohol on a fresh cut. "What is happening?"

It took me a minute to process. Then, I just knew. Someone had raped me last night. Holy hell . . . Someone had *raped* me last night. I got up and washed my hands, staring at myself in the mirror. How? How had that happened?

My legs shook as I hobbled into my bedroom. I braced myself on my mattress and sat down on my bed. I winced when my body touched the sheets.

Minutes later, KG called. We talked every morning while she drove her little one to school.

My hand shook as I answered and brought the phone to my ear.

"Good morning, sleeping beauty," she cooed in my ear.

"Hi," I squeaked as I choked back tears.

"Oh no, what's wrong?" she asked.

"I'm so dumb." My head dropped to my chest. "You're going to be so mad at me."

"You are not dumb," her voice was firm. "Tell me." She said with more compassion and love.

"I hung out with some people yesterday." I swallowed hard and ran through the night's events. "One of them got me a couple drinks, then we all came back to my patio."

"Okaaay." She seemed hesitant. "That all sounds fine."

Yeah, it was fine until it wasn't. "They ended up doing cocaine on my table."

"They did WHAT!" There was no hesitation now.

"The whole group was here for a while, and my brain is fuzzy. I think . . . something happened. It hurts so much when I go to the bathroom." Tears slid down my face. In between gasps for breath, I whispered, "I think I was raped last night."

"Oh, boo. No." She almost broke down too. "I'm so sorry. What can I do?"

"Nothing." My body shook as I cried harder. "I don't know." I had no handbook for this. Oh, no. Work. Was I going to call in sick for this? I couldn't. It was a Thursday. Staff meeting day. I pushed last night away as best as I could. "I just need to get through today," I told her and myself.

"Okay. You know I'm here for you, right? I love you," she said.

I nearly crawled upstairs to my home office. Like a dazed robot, I pressed the power button on my laptop. Physically, I could work. So I should, right? My head pounded, but I needed the distraction. I replied to emails. But when I joined the virtual staff meeting, my stomach lurched. I grabbed my wastebasket and pulled it in front of me. I could not throw up in front of my team. I shut the camera off and put my head down, hovering over the garbage can.

Somehow, I made it through the entire call. Then I logged off for the day and trudged downstairs and out the back door. I turned toward the patio and noticed a cell phone charger and lighter on the table. My legs buckled, and I fell to the concrete and sobbed.

That afternoon, I reached out to Jacob. We'd been friends since our backup-dancing, drag pageant days. Years ago, when my friend Josh had been the choreographer at the Sun Prairie Civic

Theater—where I'd been in a few shows—he'd introduced me to Jacob and to the world of drag.

I started the video call but could barely look at myself on the screen. My eyes were so red and puffy.

"Oh honey, what's up?" His big blue eyes pierced through the screen, and his brow furrowed the second he saw my face.

If I didn't tell him immediately, I wouldn't be able to say the words. My throat burned, and my eyes filled with tears. "I was raped last night."

"What?" His mouth dropped, and he covered it with his hand.

I told him what I remembered.

"Jaimie, I'm so sorry this happened to you." He paused and rested his chin on his hands. "Are you going to report it?"

My throat tightened. I hadn't thought that far ahead. "I don't know."

"This is a decision only you can make. But I hope you can do whatever you need to get through this."

"Thank you so much. I love you," I told him.

"I love you, too," he said.

Minutes after our call ended, Nicole called to let me know that Otis never showed to see the house. He was supposed to meet her here. Wow. I'd completely forgotten that was this afternoon. Guess I had other things on my mind.

I accepted the consolation. As if what had happened the night before wasn't bad enough, the entire group knew where I lived. They could literally come back any time. I took a deep breath and told her about the rape.

"Oh no. I don't want to believe he's capable of this. But one night a while back, I saw Otis out at a neighborhood bar. He was hitting on someone, and I could tell she wasn't into it. I had the bartender kick him out."

Why hadn't she said anything about that last night? I took a deep breath and squeaked into the phone, "Oh."

After a short pause, she encouraged me to report it.

"I don't know," I stammered. "I don't remember it happening. I don't need to report it to get through it."

"I totally get that. And you get to decide. But I believe whoever did this to you, it's not the first time, and it won't be the last."

Well, when she put it that way, I needed to report it. Not for me but for other women.

I called Jess on my way to the hospital. I needed a calming force as I drove. I parked and told her I'd update her along the way. She texted before I reached the main entrance.

Jess: Love you <heart emojis> <rainbow emojis> Do you need someone there?

Me: No, but thanks for asking.

Jess: Ok. Please let me know if you need or want me there.

Me: I will. It's like you're here with me already.

I checked in and told the nurse why I was there. Not exactly where I wanted to be on a child-free Thursday night. I couldn't believe this had happened to me. I felt like a narrator in a movie—someone else's movie. My knees bounced up and down repeatedly. My heart beat faster. How painful was the exam going to be? I reminded myself why I was there. Maybe I could prevent even one other person from going through it. I exhaled, and my heartbeat slowed a bit. I mindlessly scrolled on my phone for over two hours while I waited to be called.

Finally, a forensic nurse appeared and asked me to follow her.

My legs shook the entire way to the exam room. I sat on the edge of my chair and told her about last night.

The nurse listened and took notes. She left the room long enough for me to change into a gown and knocked before she came back in.

My phone buzzed.

Jess: Are you still there?

Me: Yes, about to start the exam.

Jess: I see your pain, and it's big. I also see your courage, and it's bigger. You can do hard things. – Glennon Doyle

Me: I was thinking of that exact phrase earlier.

The nurse was kind and compassionate as she examined me.

Tears slid down my cheeks as she swabbed and photographed every inch of my body. I had bruises all over my legs.

"Do you want to see the pictures?" she asked.

I did, and I didn't. I needed to see my body through her eyes. "Yes," I replied.

She showed me the cuts and bruises on the small screen of her camera. She explained petechiae—the dot-like spots you get on your skin from bleeding.

I recognized the word from *Law and Order: SVU*. I felt like I already knew the answer, but I wanted her to confirm it. I needed to hear her say the words. "I was raped?"

"I can't be sure because I wasn't there. But I do see significant injuries consistent with sexual assault."

A punch to my gut. Even though I expected that, my brain wasn't prepared for it.

The forensic nurse asked if I wanted to report the case officially.

Duh. Exactly. Wasn't that why I was here? I had to take the next step and agree to share my story with the police. I sat and shivered. On standby once again.

About twenty minutes later, the nurse entered the exam room with a police officer on her shoulder. He looked at me with sad eyes. "Can you tell me what happened to you last night?" He pulled out a notepad.

Once again, I recounted my story. I felt robotic, like I was spitting out facts for a test. I mentioned my dress, the phone charger, and lighter.

The officer stopped writing. "Would you be able to bring those items, plus your underwear and sheets to the station tomorrow?"

Those idiots had left their DNA for testing. I almost laughed. "Absolutely."

I felt strong. I needed to do this to prevent it from happening to anyone else. I answered a few more questions, the whole time wondering how one human could assault another human that way?

Burning with rage and almost in a daze, I left and somehow found my car in the parking garage. My brain felt empty on the drive home.

I felt like a zombie as I put the dress, sheets, lighter, and phone charger into a bag. Where were my underwear though? I trudged down to the laundry room in the basement. Bingo. I picked them up off the floor and noticed a dark red spot in the crotch. I stepped backward, as if I'd been punched in the stomach. Courtesy of chemotherapy, I hadn't had a period in almost two years. I steadied myself and turned back toward the stairs. Within minutes, I collapsed into bed and fell asleep.

Hours later, my phone buzzed. The sun had just started to rise.

Jess: How can I help? Do you want porch coffee today? Did you sleep at all?

Me: Some. But not really.

Jess: I can be there before ten. What's your coffee order? I'll have a mask and meet you outside.

Me: You're an amazing friend. Can I have a chai tea latte? *iced* chai tea latte.

Jess: That I remember.

Me: Offfff course you do. Thank you so much.

Ten minutes after nine, Jess appeared at my door with that nectar of the gods in a plastic cup. We gave each other a masked hug, and I cried on her shoulder. Given what had happened one night earlier, social distance rules be damned.

After she left, I opened my contacts on my phone. Magali and I had been trying to catch up for a little while. I'd joined her front and center table for countless drag shows at FIVE. She'd also given me her shoulder to cry on after an emotional night at Pride Prom. After I drained my latte, I texted her with a bit more urgency.

Me: Any chance you can talk now? I wouldn't ask if it weren't important.

Magali: Of course!

Within minutes, she called, and I described the last forty-eight hours.

Magali appeared on my porch during her lunch break with a masked hug and a bag of chocolate kisses.

At that point, those were the only kisses I could handle.

Chapter Four

RELIEF

THE NEXT DAY, NICOLE called and jumped right into what I needed to hear—that we had a very interested buyer for the house.

At the exact same time, COVID cases skyrocketed. And I slunk back into my hole.

I crept out only for masked trips to the grocery store.

Within three hours, the buyer sent an offer with a July 9th closing date. YAASSSSS!!

I had five-and-a-half weeks to find another place to live. Not so yaassss.

Even if I found a three-bedroom apartment, it wouldn't have the same amount of space as a three-bedroom house with a mostly finished basement. The kids and I needed to pare down. In the hallway outside my office, I looked at shelves filled with Lego creations. Sure, they were cool. They also had a layer of dust an inch thick.

My fifteen-year-old son walked by my office.

I leaned my head outside the door and called, "Hey, do you still want these Lego sets?"

"Uhhhh . . ." He stopped in front of the middle shelf.

I knew that he didn't answer vague questions well. "How about you pick two or three sets to keep, and I'll sell the rest?"

"Okay." He grabbed his two favorites.

I posted them online, and the messages poured in. I was pleasantly surprised to read one from a friend I'd taught with before we'd both had children.

Andrea: I would love these sets. Mine is a *Star Wars* junky right now!

Me: 100% yours

Andrea: Should we swing by this evening? It'll be good to see you!

Me: Absolutely!

I carefully placed the Lego sets in a plastic bag and set the bag outside my office. My phone buzzed repeatedly. Enough, people. The toys were spoken for.

Wait, this was a phone call from the City of Madison. A sixth sense told me to answer it.

"This is Detective Lindsey with the Madison Police Department. Is this Jaimie?"

I confirmed, and she asked if I remembered anything else. I wished I did.

She explained that my case was unique because it could be one or more people in a group. They would test the DNA on the items they left behind, then request a sample from each of the men. "This will make the process take longer. And we're backed up because of COVID."

Really? I had literally hand-delivered their genetic material to you. I made a fist and slowly opened it. This wasn't her fault. The system was broken. I thanked her for calling me and hung up. I set my phone down and returned to my work inbox. Focus. I had a friend's visit to look forward to.

Andrea arrived a couple hours later, and we visited from a distance.

She peeked inside the bag. "The kids are going to love these!"

"I'm so glad." And I was. Someone's kids should use them.

"So, moving?" She pushed up her sunglasses.

"Yeah, it's time," I told her. "But we're staying in Madison."

"Well, good luck," she offered.

I definitely needed that luck as I scoured for apartments every day. If only I wanted a studio or one-bedroom and a move-in date of August 1.

About a week later, I met up with Adam for a socially distanced visit. After catching up for a bit, I blurted out, "I don't know where we're going to live."

He immediately said, "You can move in with me. It'd be fun."

Awwwww. What a sweet and generous offer. But no. Sure, it'd be great for a month or so. We'd have a blast and get completely caught up on *RuPaul's Drag Race*. But two weeks of that time would include two teenagers. In his two-bedroom place. That was too many twos. Nope. Nope. And nope.

Desperate, I posted on social media next: *Anyone have any 3-bedroom apartment connections for me? Looking for availability on July 1. Thank you!!!!!!!!!!*

A couple friends commented but gave no new information. That night I heard from Andrea.

Andrea: I saw your post about apartments. If you get stuck (or find the apartment of your dreams that isn't available until August) and need a place to stay, our house will be empty in July. You and the kids could stay here... you'd just have to water my plants!

Once again, a friend stepped up for me and my family.

On the hottest day of the summer, Ben, Phoenix, Lacie, Brandon, and Magali all showed up ready to work. We carried everything out of my house—and somehow fit it into a U-Haul—while keeping our distance from each other. Pesky pandemic.

I drove the truck to Andrea's house, gripping the steering wheel on the highway. If someone heard me breathing, they would have guessed I was headed for labor and delivery.

Minutes after I parked, my friend Amanda arrived with her husband and son. Right after I carried three boxes into the garage and lost steam, Andrea's neighbor ran across the street to help. Perfect timing. Praise the energy of youth!

After a month in Andrea's beautiful home, I moved again. Because Brandon and Lacie were overachievers, they showed up again. Another Brandon, a queen who performed as Bianca at FIVE, helped too.

I adjusted to apartment living slowly but surely. The mask mandate required everyone to wear one in the hallways, stairwells, and on the elevators. So much for getting to know my new neighbors. At least I'd really get to know who had crow's feet.

I focused on getting to know my neighborhood instead. Just behind the building, I'd gained a bike path to the lakeshore edge of campus. Less than five minutes away sat three beautiful tennis courts. The last time I'd hit a tennis ball was in high school. I was going to take this seriously. But first, I needed a cute tennis skirt. I mean, how could I show up in boring shorts? I drove to the sporting goods store and found my perfect match. Way too excited after wearing it, I posted on social media.

I will now only go by my tennis skirt's name, Blazing Cherry Leopard.

My friends shared my excitement. One really took it to heart.

Jess: Amazing. Changing it in my contacts now . . .

Another boon to that summer? Patio drag shows. Summer turned to fall, and my anxiety ramped up.

There still wasn't a vaccine. What happened when it got cold? I needed the drag shows for as long as possible. I needed people. I wasn't doing well without people. I'd sit in an igloo if I had to.

In another nod from the universe, heat lamps were set up around the patio at FIVE. Two of my worlds colliding, I reminisced about high school football games as I sat huddled under a blanket, wearing a coat, hat, and gloves. Although, I'd never had boozy hot cocoa or apple cider back in high school.

I enjoyed fall so much that I hadn't thought about the rape case in months. Until Lindsey texted on a cool early October afternoon.

Lindsey: Please give me a call when time allows so that I can provide you an update on your case.

I hit the call button within seconds.

After quick pleasantries, she explained that DNA evidence cleared both Otis and Dylan.

I blinked multiple times and opened and closed my mouth. I didn't know what to say. I couldn't have predicted her update if I'd tried. I felt relieved to be moving forward.

"We're having a hard time reaching Jack," she said, "but we'll keep trying."

Jack. Shocker. My head felt like a teapot ready to shoot steam from my ears. I paused and collected myself before I spoke and thanked her for the update.

Good thing I'd found a new sport that let me work through some aggression.

On every mild fall day, I played tennis with my son. He was into it, and I was thrilled for the fun form of exercise. One afternoon, I bent down to pick up the ball, and a bolt of electricity shot down my leg, setting my nerves on fire.

What the hell was that?

I knew I'd been sitting more during the pandemic, but I was still active. The pain stuck around. I felt it jolt through me when I sat down to tie my shoe. Then my back pulsed while I slept. I didn't know what to do. I'd never dealt with back pain. Maybe I just really needed a massage. It had been at least a year since I'd had one. I thought about going to a massage therapist with a mask on and panicked. Would I really be able to relax lying face down breathing into my mask? I decided no.

During a staff meeting one day, I posed the question to the team. "My back hurts all the time. I don't want to get a massage. Does anybody have any other ideas?"

My friend and work teammate Katie gave me an immediate solution. "How about a chiropractor?"

Facepalm. Why had that not even crossed my mind? Could I blame pandemic brain?

On October 27, 2020, I visited a new-to-me chiropractor ten minutes away. I felt relief with the first adjustment.

Chapter Five

BACK TO THE APP

H ave you ever watched a show and related so much to a character that you wondered if the writers lived in your brain? Me neither. Just kidding. An empath, I could relate to a fictitious life story from a thirty-second ad.

In early 2021, I was back in a bit of a hole. A vaccine didn't exist yet, patio drag shows were a bittersweet memory, and I stayed home by myself. A lot. To escape my reality, I traveled to Los Angeles, circa 2004. I quickly fell in love with *The L Word*. The characters' lives intrigued and inspired me.

By the early spring of 2021, my back hurt every day. I no longer felt relief with my chiropractor visits. I whined and cried to KG on the phone.

"Do you want to try a mattress topper?" she asked.

"I guess I could," I said through tears. "But if that's not it, then I've wasted money I don't have on it . . ."

"They're not that expensive. And I can do the search, read all the reviews, and find the best one for you. I got you."

"I know you do," I said and cried some more. What did people do without friends?

I loved KG's enthusiasm for a mattress topper. But negative thoughts about my back pain swirled around my brain. I kept thinking it wasn't about my sleeping situation. That there had to be a medical reason. I needed to check in with a doctor. Wasn't it convenient when your soulmate happened to be one?

That afternoon, I talked to Adam on the phone as I walked around the neighborhood. "What if my cancer is back, and it's spreading through my body?"

"Jaimie, it could be anything," he replied.

"And if you say it's me getting older, I will punch you in the face," I warned him.

He laughed. "I wasn't going to say that."

I chuckled too and felt myself relax. I already had an appointment scheduled for routine bloodwork. If there was anything to be concerned about, I'd find out then from my oncologist. In the meantime, I added a dating app to my phone. A bad back shouldn't keep me from finding romance, right?

Near the end of April, I drove to the clinic for routine bloodwork. I mindlessly scrolled the app while I waited to see my oncologist. All routine. There hadn't been any surprises since spring 2018. I wasn't expecting any now.

Dr. Milliken entered the exam room and shook my hand. "Great news, your bloodwork looks good."

"That is great news," I smiled.

Then Dr. Milliken asked the million-dollar questions. "So, what else is going on? How are you doing?"

"Well, my back hurts all the time," I said, like it wasn't a big deal.

"Oh." Some concern crossed his face. "That's not good. Let's do an MRI and see what's going on."

My brain hopped in a DeLorean and traveled back to 2018 as I thought about tests—waiting to get in for them and then waiting for the results.

Thanks to the schedulers, I got an appointment in two weeks. Okay, fine. I'd been in pain for months. What was two more weeks? I messaged Adam after my appointment.

Me: Blood work is good. He does want me to have an MRI for my back. Just to be safe.

Adam: Why your back?

Me: Because it still hurts. He's concerned. Especially with weekly chiro visits.

Adam: It's best to be safe!!

I returned to my home office, ready to work. I responded to one email and heard my phone buzz. Maybe Adam had more questions. I flipped my phone over and read *Lindsey, MPD.* Oh no. What did she want?

She wanted to update me on the case. They'd tracked down Jack, who had secured a lawyer. Rage welled inside me. He had someone dedicated to helping him get away with this?

"He submitted to a DNA test," Lindsey said. "And the case goes to the DA's office next."

I stared out the window, unable to speak.

"Do you have any questions," she asked.

I stoically said, "No."

"Before we go, I have a couple questions for you." Lindsey's tone hovered between tentative and businesslike.

I scrunched up my forehead. What could she possibly need to ask me now? I wanted to fully cooperate. "Of course, go ahead."

"Do you remember anything else from that night?"

"No, I've told you everything I remembered."

"Did you have any drugs in your system?"

Um, like what? "Well, I told you already that I had alcohol."

"Anything else?"

Oh, should I have mentioned my cancer-related prescriptions? That never crossed my mind. "I take this drug called Tamoxifen, but it's part of my treatment plan."

"The lab ran your toxicology report, and they found cocaine in your system."

"They found *what*?" I felt violated all over again, then quickly shifted to feeling vindicated. "They asked me if I wanted some. I remember that, and declining, quite clearly."

"Okay, I just needed to check, in case you remembered differently. I also want you to know that this still might move slowly. The DA reviews the case, the evidence, and decides whether to charge him or not."

I didn't bother asking how long it might take from here. I hung up and set my phone back on my desk. I wiggled the computer mouse and entered my password. Jack had already taken enough from me. I refused to give him another second of my workday.

After a sound night of sleep, I woke up to a match on a dating app.

Lily: Hi, Jaimie! How wonderful to wake up and see that we matched. Your smile is crazy-amazing.

Not a bad start, I'd say.

Lily and I messaged back and forth for a week. We learned about each other's work and personal lives. For our first date, we met for tea downtown. The weather gave us an unseasonably warm day at the end of April. I found Lily sitting in the sun on State Street. We talked about our children and big goals for our lives. I shared about my cancer journey. I enjoyed her company, and our conversation flowed easily. By the time we said goodbye for the evening, we had another date set for tacos and margaritas. Easy, breezy.

What I wouldn't give for easy, breezy with my insurance company. Turns out, they didn't find an

MRI medically necessary. I wanted to blow up the universe. Not medically necessary? Because I liked to have MRIs for fun? Other than routine bloodwork as a cancer survivor and too many sinus infections, I was healthy. It's not like I requested expensive exams every week. I begged for an appointment, and here's what I got from the scheduler. "Insurance will not approve the MRI. They will approve a bone scan and a bone x-ray."

"Can I do the MRI anyway?" I asked.

"You can. But you're required to sign a form saying that if insurance denies it again, you are willing to pay for it yourself."

"How much is an MRI?"

"About six thousand," the scheduler answered.

Six what? Absolutely not. No way.

Meanwhile, Lily and I kept in touch daily. We went on three dates in ten days. We messaged every morning, before bed, and sometimes during the day. The day of my bone scan, she texted me.

Lily: How's your day going?

Me: It's going okay. I have my scan today, so I was a bit of a train wreck this morning. How's your day going?

Lily: So, fill me in, if you don't mind. What are they able to see from the scan? Has your cancer metastasized? (We can also talk about this in person rather than text.) How is your health now?

Me: I don't mind. The scan will hopefully give an answer about my back pain. It's possible the cancer has spread. My health is good. Bloodwork was solid at last check. But the back pain isn't going away, and it's concerning (to me and my oncologist). So, we'll see.

Lily: Thank you for sharing, and please keep me in the loop. I know it's early on, but I want to be there for you in any way you'd like me to be.

Dr. Milliken called three days later with the results. "Something lit up as suspicious on the bone scan."

Not what I wanted to hear. Suspicious wasn't good, unless you were watching a *Scooby Doo* marathon. "Okay, what does that mean?"

"The good news is that it was only one spot. Bone scans don't give specific information. It could be inflammation."

"And the bad news?" I asked.

"It could be cancer," he replied. "We're going to schedule that MRI."

Only a month after he'd originally requested it.

Lily came over to my place for our fifth date. I needed a change. I couldn't afford restaurants as often as we went. I cooked for her, which was intimidating. I was a master at brunch food. All bets were off for anything else.

I guess it didn't scare her off. After dinner she asked if she could say she was my girlfriend. I was excited to be in my first relationship with a woman. And my first relationship since my ex-husband.

She committed to us quickly. At least, it seemed that way from her texts a week later.

Lily: How was your night out? Also, what's your ring size?

I fed off her excitement. I wanted everyone to know about us. I started with my son while I washed the dinner dishes. "You've heard me say I might want to be in a relationship with a woman, right?"

"Yeah, I heard that." He looked up from the Brewer's game.

"Well, I have a girlfriend now."

"How long has that been happening?" He didn't seem to be freaked out.

"We started talking a month ago, but I didn't want to say anything until it was more serious. Now it is," I explained.

"Gotcha." He turned his head back to the game.

I told my older teen when they got home after a night out with friends. They also asked how long it had been going on. Geez, nosey. Then I told my ex.

"Oh," he said, with a hint of surprise. "That's great. I wish you well."

Before I went to bed, I texted Lily.

Me: I told the kids and their dad about you, well us.

Lily: That's the best news ever! You made my day, my year, my life. I'm proud of you. <heart emoji>

And to think, I thought Pride was next month.

Chapter Six

FAVORITE FLOWER?

A couple of days later, I had an unexpected child-free night. On an unrelated note, congratulations to the Milwaukee Bucks on your outstanding playoff run.

That night, Lily and I met at one of her favorite neighborhood restaurants. The sun set as we chatted, shared an appetizer, and sipped on fancy, handcrafted cocktails.

After we finished, we strolled around the corner, and I saw the most beautiful flowering plant. I stopped short. I needed to capture this moment. "Can we take a picture together?" I asked.

She agreed with a smile.

After a few attempts, we took a social-media-worthy selfie.

"Would you be okay with me posting this and tagging you tonight?" I asked. Why wait? The kids knew. Why not tell everybody? I posted our picture and added the caption: "I'd like everyone to meet my girlfriend, Lily."

With over five hundred reactions of love and happiness, I nearly broke the internet. I had no idea people would be this excited.

Five days later, Lily's first message of the day threw me.

Lily: Do you think you could grow to truly love me?

Ummm, where was this coming from?

Me: Absolutely. I feel more strongly about you every day.

I drove to visit my dear friend Kate that day. She and I had taught at the same school in the early 2000s. While I was there, I took a couple pictures of a cool cave and sent them to Lily. She didn't respond. I thought she was upset with me, but I couldn't figure out why. The next morning, she cleared things up.

Lily: Morning, Jaimie. I'm not angry, but I need to know why we're toying at a relationship when it's obvious that you're not attracted to me or interested in knowing anything about who I am. I understand if you just want to explore something new, but I'd really appreciate it if you'd be honest about what you're looking for.

Sobbing, I called her immediately. I cried through most of the phone call. According to Lily, I wasn't a loving person. Or at least, I didn't know how to show others I loved them.

"Sometimes, you just want to hear 'you take my breath away,'" she told me.

How could I respond to that? Let's be real. There is one person I might say that to. And if you read my first book, you know that's Serena van der Woodsen from *Gossip Girl*. At a complete loss for words, I didn't stay on the phone much longer.

I needed to get out of my head. Best place to do that? At the White Party with Adam. I first learned about the White Party during the first episode of the second season of *Gossip Girl*. My girlfriend Serena had slayed as a Grecian goddess.

Adam picked me up, and we were on our way. About five minutes from my place, he stopped at a light.

I heard the crunch before I felt the impact that jerked my body forward.

In the sideview mirror, I saw that the car behind us had been crushed between us and a minivan. Adam and I got out of the car, both of us in head-to-toe white. He checked on everyone, and they seemed okay. But the car in the middle needed major repairs.

The third driver, who'd caused the accident, cried into her phone.

"Well, at least I have a reason for my back hurting now," I whispered to Adam and shivered.

"I can't with you," he replied.

Later that night at FIVE, I visited with Casey. I'd met him a year earlier during a game of darts, and we'd immediately struck up a deep conversation. While I didn't see him out often, I was always happy when I did. We hadn't caught up in a long time.

Behind me, Adam said, "Who doesn't lock their phone?"

What was he talking about? I ignored him.

Then he reached over and handed me my phone.

I looked down to see a side-by-side collage of the two of us on New Year's Eve 2019 and earlier that evening. Oh. Me. I didn't lock my phone. But hey, if your friend hijacks your phone and only adds a really cool picture like that, you've got an awesome friend.

While I listened to Casey, one of my favorite songs started. I moved just a bit to the beat.

"I can't believe you're not on the dance floor right now," Adam said.

"Bitch, I AM the dance floor," I told him.

All he could do was laugh.

After a night of dancing and sleeping in, Adam and I met at the Union.

He wanted to talk about Lily. "I have concerns." He pantomimed unrolling a long scroll of paper in front of me. "You should still be in the honeymoon phase," he explained. "This should be a happy time. And you are spending so much time crying."

Okay, valid points.

The next day, Dr. Milliken called about my MRI results. "There's a spot on L5 of your spine. I think that's cancer . . ."

"And?" My stomach flipflopped. Here we go again. "I feel like there's more."

"The spots on your liver are nebulous. I'm very worried," he continued.

No. This wasn't happening. He never said he was worried before. And now he was very worried? I took a breath to calm myself. "So, what's next?"

"It needs to be proven." His head dropped, and his voice became more serious, if that was even possible. "But I'm rarely surprised. The spots are 95% likely to be cancer."

I mustered a very soft, "Okay."

"Are you feeling numbness in your feet or legs?" he asked.

Why would I be feeling that? My heart started to race. Was this some kind of trick question? "No, not that I know of."

"There could be a tumor in the lining around your spinal cord. It could start to cause problems quickly. I want you to visit the radiation oncologist tomorrow."

I couldn't argue with that plan. I worked half a day and headed to the hospital for a CT scan. I had some hills to conquer walking there, but they beat the massive parking ramp any day. Another day, another test. And more waiting.

During the wait, Lily hung out with the kids and me. She came over to celebrate my son's birthday. That night, she texted me.

Lily: I cannot possibly tell you how much I enjoy hanging out with the fam. You've raised a couple of beautiful human beings!

I read that and liked the idea of us spending more time together. We talked about me visiting the zoo that weekend while she worked at the ice cream shop there. Adam's words loomed in the back of my mind. I decided to hold onto hope. Maybe Lily and I were returning to the honeymoon phase?

Saturday rolled around, and it was chores and groceries. Then my son got sucked into a puzzle. I told Lily about our day, but I guess I wasn't clear enough about not stopping by the zoo.

Lily: Are you guys still thinking of popping by? I'll be busy closing soon, but I have a good forty-five minutes to spend until then.

Me: We're going to come for ice cream tomorrow. He is so laser focused on this puzzle!

We messaged a few more times, but I still felt like something was off. The next morning, I tried to get answers.

Me: Good morning, Beautiful! I've been thinking about you nonstop. Wondering what you're thinking and feeling. I understand you're at work and hope it's going well so far. I'm looking forward to seeing you there later. And hopefully, we can talk tonight?

Lily: Good morning! It's good to know that you've been thinking of me. I'm just missing you and wishing we had enough time behind us for the depth of relationship I hope to have with you one day. It'll be great to see you guys if you decide to pop by. And, yes, I'm happy to talk tonight if you'd like.

Wait one second. "If" we decide to pop by. Didn't I say we were going to stop by? A half hour later, my phone buzzed again.

Lily: The days you love me feel so incredibly good, which makes the ones where you're not feeling it a little hard.

That night I called her. "I'm trying to understand how you don't feel loved."

"I was waiting all day yesterday to see you at the zoo, and you never came," she answered.

"I thought it was clear that I might not make it from our messages during the day, but I realize I wasn't," I said.

"Can I come to your appointment this week?" she asked.

Sidenote: I almost always went to appointments alone. I had since 2018. Not that I didn't want company. I simply felt confident in my ability to listen and take notes on my own. And in certain appointments, another person couldn't even be with you.

I thought for a moment which appointment I had next. "This week it's a scan. I'll walk to the hospital, sit in a machine for thirty to forty-five minutes, then walk home." I lived eight-tenths of a mile away. It would take me far longer to drive.

"So, I guess you just want me to stay out of your way next week then?" she asked.

"That's not what I'm saying. How about dinner that night? You could see me and the kids, and that would be super helpful to me that afternoon," I offered.

"I'll try and figure something out," she replied.

"Thank you. Okay, time for me to head to bed soon. I love you."

The next morning, I didn't hear from her at all. I saw her as I walked up to the ice cream shop in the zoo, as she hurried away to handle an inventory emergency. That night, I called again. I hadn't enjoyed most of our phone call the night before. I was also exhausted from a full weekend of chores and errand running with teenagers. But I dialed her number anyway.

She asked how I was doing, and I complained about the kids for a bit. She was a mom too. She could relate.

"If they annoy you that much, why don't you ask their dad to have them full-time?" she asked.

Was. She. Kidding. Me? I could not put words together. She wanted me to give up my kids?

"You just really enjoy your time without them. I get it. You're a party girl," she continued.

My skin felt hot, like I'd been thrown into an active volcano. I'd never wanted to hang up the phone on someone more in my life.

"I want you to be happy. If you just want to not have the kids and go out dancing all the time, do that," she finished.

I chose to not dignify her thoughts with a response. I switched gears. "I feel like I can't give you what you need. I'm just not a romantic person with my words," I explained.

"It's okay. I don't need that from you. I have other people who talk to me like that," she countered.

Wait, what? "This is something that's really important to you. You're just never going to get that from your partner?" I asked her.

"I don't need it from you," she replied.

"That feels awful to me. To know that you need something, and I can never meet that need. I will feel terrible every day."

"Well, it seems like you don't want this relationship to go further." She paused. "I enjoyed getting to know you, and you got rid of your man residue. We'll just leave it at that," she concluded.

That was it? I went from the "love of your life" to "let's put a pin in it" pretty quickly. In shock, I mumbled, "Okay, take care." And ended the call.

My phone buzzed not a minute later.

New post by Lily. She shared a picture of us smiling next to each other in our rollerblades and wrote the caption: "The other day, Jaimie and I embarked upon the I Am the Storm Challenge. When you're with your true love, even shredded wheels and skinned knees seem auspicious."

One of her friends quickly commented. "Ya'll so cute. Skinned knees and all!"

Lily: I think so, too. Unfortunately, Jaimie just let me know that she doesn't quite have the feels for yours truly. I must say, I am grateful for the illusion, however brief in duration.

Lily's friend: oh, I'm so sorry, hon. ☹

Lily: Thanks. I kept feeling as though something was off, but she always assured me she loved me. Next time, I'll listen to my gut. It's all good! After all, I have you guys.

Turns out lilies were not my new favorite flower.

Chapter Seven

KILLING IT

AFTER THINGS ENDED WITH Lily, I thought I was ready to move on. My brain running nonstop at 5 a.m. told a different story. So, what did I do to quiet the constant din inside my head? Message Adam, of course.

Me: 5 a.m. struggles, Jaimie edition

1. Why couldn't I accept her being so in love with me?

2. What if no one feels this strongly about me again?

3. Maybe I don't want a relationship, I'm just telling myself I do.

Adam:

1. Because it was crazy, over the top, and not genuine. She was in love with you so you would be in love with her. Because she needed to be in love.

2. She did not feel that strongly about you. IF she did, she would not have said hurtful things.

3. She was ingenuine and fake. And maybe you don't want a relationship. And if that's the case, that's fine.

Me: Yeah, I'm not sure now. I feel like if I do something casual, I want more of the person. I try to have a relationship, and I can't give them all the attention they want/need.

Adam: She told you that. You cannot believe what she told you. She is CRAZY. CRAAAAZY.

Later in the day, I received a notification that Lily posted. Oh boy. I clenched my jaw and clicked.

She wrote: Perhaps it is the commitment we make to ourselves that matters most. Underneath her bit of wisdom, she shared a picture focusing on her hands. With a ring on her index finger.

Subtle, Lily. Very subtle.

Enough about her. My brain turned its attention to cancer center appointments. Later that week, I sat across from Dr. Milliken in one of the usual exam rooms to talk about the PET scan.

"There are three spots on the liver that light up." He looked down briefly. "The biggest is golf-ball size."

I felt like a golf club hit me in the stomach. Nothing the size of a golf ball should be inside of me. With that pause, I knew there was more. I tightened my fingers around the edge of my chair. "Continue."

"There's one spot on your L5, one spot underneath your mastectomy scar, and mildly enlarged lymph nodes near your liver," he said.

No. This wasn't happening. I felt queasy and squeezed my eyes shut. I slowly opened my eyes and looked directly into his. "What do we do with all of that?"

"I'm still not 100% sure. I need a biopsy to know if this is cancer or not."

"Okay," I agreed, and we set up an appointment.

That Friday, I met with the radiation oncologist again. I hadn't seen her since the summer of 2019. All the days I'd spent in the basement of the hospital felt like a distant memory. I sat in the empty exam room, grateful for the quiet.

She knocked on the door and opened it just enough to fit her body through. She sat across from me, and we caught up and visited like old friends. "I want to start radiation with the calculated risk that your breast cancer is back again," she explained.

"Okayyy," I trailed off, confused. Why would I go through radiation if they weren't even sure I had cancer?

"The tumor growing around your spine could start to grow on the nearby nerves. I'm concerned about potential paralysis. Radiation is for pain control and to protect your nerves."

"Okay, let's do it." At this point, moving at all was painful.

The oncologist recommended five days of radiation, starting next week.

On Monday, I drove back to the cancer center for my needle biopsy. I met with a new nurse, Aaron. After he confirmed my entire medical history, we visited. He told me about his wife and why they'd moved to Madison. I shared about my first book coming out.

Aaron led me back to the ultrasound room. Two ultrasound techs worked to find the right spot to biopsy.

"Can you roll onto your side," the first tech asked.

"Mmhmm." I slowly pushed myself up with my hands and winced. Rolling from one side to the other felt like an Olympic event.

"Your back, right?" Aaron yelled from his computer in the corner of the exam room.

"Yeah." I barely croaked out the answer.

The ultrasound tech sweetly offered, "We could probably try again and get it with you on your back."

Awwww, hell no. I did not want to have this procedure a second time. I needed you to do it right this time. I managed to say, "No, that's okay." For some reason, I felt the need to reassure everyone in the room. "I can handle it." I gripped the sheet next to my thigh. "I'm tough." <Insert tiny pause here> "And I cry a lot."

Cue a roomful of laughter.

That Friday, I started radiation. Only five days this time. I say only because in 2018, I'd had six weeks of radiation. I ended up in the same room as the last time, shellshocked. The ceiling tile painted with a leafy tree brought me right back to Central Park like it had in 2018.

After my second day, I met with Dr. Milliken. "Jaimie, I can now confirm that you have metastatic breast cancer."

Without anyone touching a light switch, the room went dark. Here we were again. Part of me had expected this outcome. The other part of me sat in disbelief. Stunned, I didn't move a muscle. But in my mind, I shook my head and stomped like an insolent toddler. No no no no no. I already went through this. Not again. Pass. Finally, my rational brain took over, and I finished my internal temper tantrum and relaxed my shoulders.

Everything added up to this point. Weeks ago, Dr. Milliken had been 95% sure that my cancer had come back. No amount of loud outbursts or pity parties changed the current facts. Three years ago, I trusted my medical team to take care of me. They'd mapped out a course of treatment and saved my life. I believed they could do it again. My next step? Listen, learn, and buckle up. "What's the plan?"

"There are a number of options. IV chemo every three weeks. I'll check the availability of clinical trials in Madison. There are also a couple chemo pills," he explained.

Déjà vu all over again. I sighed. Losing my hair again. Losing my sense of taste again. Losing my choices again. Needing to tell my kids I had cancer. Again. I inhaled and let out all I could. "Okay."

He set his hand on my shoulder. "Think of this like a marathon." His tone was encouraging. "It's not curable, but it is treatable."

Hadn't I told everyone that I was done with marathons? I'd run the Chicago Marathon in 2012. While I was grateful for the experience, I'd vowed it to be my one and only.

I drove home and called my amazing friend Jen. We'd met in college through church and ended up singing backup in a band together. For most of the last decade though, she hosted me in her New York City home for a long weekend once a year. I needed her radiant energy and sage wisdom. She delivered, as I expected. After we said goodbye, my phone buzzed with a new text.

Jen: If travel is what you need, you know you're 100% welcome <heart emoji> <flamenco dancer emoji>

I required this like oxygen. In 2013, after one of the greatest weekends of my entire life, I promised myself I would visit New York City at least once a year. I kept that promise until 2020. Thanks a lot, COVID. It had been too long. I needed to go back.

Me: Thank you so much. I do think that's what I need soon. I'll look at flights and check back with you.

I didn't find anything immediately, but the idea cemented in my brain. The next day, I laced up my sneakers and prepared to walk the hills to the hospital again. Day three of radiation. "I can do this," I confidently told myself. I felt like someone squeezed a vise grip around my spine just a little bit tighter with every step. I arrived at the hospital sweaty from exertion and sat in the waiting room for a few minutes to recover.

After I checked in and got called back, I shuffled behind the radiation tech, shivering in the air conditioning. I slowly sat down on the bed. As I reclined, I winced in pain.

The radiation technician leaned down toward me. "Are you okay?"

"Laying on my back hurts the most. That's why I'm here."

"Anything I can do?" she asked.

"Oooh, can you make a new radio station?" I was not feeling the oldies rock vibe she had playing.

"Sure, what would you like?"

"Can you type in *Only Girl in the World* by Rihanna? That should be a good station."

"I can't enter a song, but I can make a Rihanna station. Will that work?"

"Sure!"

The technician left to go to the control room.

The treatment started and so did some familiar lyrics. "It's getting late, I'm making my way over to my favorite place . . ."

I had to will my body to stay still and not dance.

Over the intercom, I heard, "This is the best DJ April can do. How is it?"

"Great. You're killing it, April!"

A short ten minutes later, treatment was over. As the other technicians helped me up, one of them asked, "How did DJ April do?"

"So good." I smiled. And I meant it. "We turnt up in here."

DJ April confirmed, "That's what we do! Killing cancer and getting turnt up."

Carbone Cancer Center, I wonder if you missed an incredible marketing opportunity with that line.

Chapter Eight

BEE . . . NINE

A WEEK LATER, MY friend Soleil arrived for a visit. We'd become friends years ago through my full-time nonprofit job. I supported athletes who fundraised to cure cancer, and she trained for the Chicago Marathon. We reconnected in 2019 when we both ran the Austin Half Marathon for the same nonprofit. Our friendship deepened over that weekend, and she wanted to see Madison. I introduced her to FIVE Nightclub, and she made fast friends. Her energy lit up every room she entered.

On Sunday, I hosted my first in-person brunch since February 2020. So very long overdue. Friends enjoyed my baked French toast—a brunch staple I served every time I hosted brunch—and it felt like old times. I bopped around the room and fed my extrovert soul.

A few friends asked about Lily. Not a surprise. I'd recently posted about our relationship. I shared where things went wrong and how Adam saw it coming a mile away.

He snapped his head at me and yelled, "Jaimie, I've been trying to politely tell you for weeks that she's crazy!"

Everyone in earshot, meaning everyone in the room, burst out laughing.

On July 8, 2021—almost three years to the day from my very first chemo treatment—I drove to the clinic at 1 South Park for chemotherapy. Talk about déjà vu all over again. I felt a sense of comfort in the familiar space. The drug names were even familiar. Taxotere, a cousin of Taxol, and Herceptin pumped into my port. The nurses had treated me like gold in 2018, would 2021 be any different? Spoiler alert, it was not.

Dr. Milliken warned me again that I'd likely lose my hair. Once again, I scheduled a proactive haircut. History repeated itself. Sort of. On the way to the salon, I held a pity party for myself. Why did I have to go through this again? Why me? I took a few deep breaths and pulled the door open wide.

My stylist Yair hugged me. "Hello, Gorgeous! What are we doing today?"

I caught him up on my situation. "With chemo, I'm going to lose my hair. Again. So can you give me a cute, short cut?"

He rested his head on my shoulder and locked eyes with mine in the mirror. "Oh, honey. I can do that. I gotchu."

I smiled weakly and sat in the chair. Afterward, I looked in the mirror. Yair had delivered. Still, I missed my hair. I looked out the window to see pouring rain. Apparently, my emotions matched the weather now. Or the other way around. At least I had a hood on my raincoat.

The entire next day while I worked in my office, I felt seasick. I sipped on ginger ale. My stomach flip flopped. I sipped some more. Everything I ate tasted passable or terrible. Thanks for messing with my taste buds again, chemo.

Hours later, I switched from work to personal emails. Yep, living the good life. It wasn't all glitz and glamour over here.

One unread email popped a single word subject line. *Contract.*

I blinked rapidly. My mouth dropped open. My hours in front of the laptop had paid off. I'd edited my first book every day for weeks that spring and early summer. And by fall, I'd be holding it in my hands. I posted my news, and the congratulatory wishes rolled in like a tidal wave.

I decided to create my own celebration and searched for flights to New York City. I found a deal the last weekend of August and texted Jen immediately. She was available to host. I barely finished reading her text and booked the flights.

Apparently, my friends wanted to keep the festive mood alive. Without asking, they started promoting the book. Adelaide and Sheeza brought me up on FIVE's stage at the halfway point of their show. Kat and the Hurricane invited me to their variety show.

One hot summer night, I attended Cynthia's drag bingo at Shamrock Bar & Grill. She asked me to share about the book and double-checked the release date. "Okay everyone, put this date into your phones. I'm waiting." She quickly returned to the bingo game and called out, "B-9."

"Thank God!" The crowd responded the way they always did.

B-9. Benign. I chuckled to myself at the irony of the cancer patient screaming benign all night.

Chapter Nine

BEAUTIFUL

THAT CUTE HAIRCUT LASTED a month. All my hair fell out by the end of August. No shame in being bald. I felt best, though, when I looked in a mirror and saw hair. I moaned to my friend Lacie about it, and she offered her cosplay wigs. Why not? My friend Caryn, who I'd met through the burlesque community, also loaned me two fabulous ombre wigs.

I felt good and wanted to spend time with friends. Chemo didn't need to keep me from that. Or so I thought.

The third Friday of August, I sat through what felt like a mundane treatment. That night, I had dinner with my friend Neal. We'd met through Adam. After dinner, I made my way to FIVE for a drag show. Not enough hours of sleep later, I had a breakfast date with my friend Kelly. We'd known each other since our kids were in kindergarten together. That night, guess where I went? You don't really have to guess.

I'll tell you. FIVE. I still felt good. Why not live my best life? The next day, I enjoyed breakfast with my favorite chemo nurse from 2018. Later, I dressed for FIVE again, pairing a cute floral strapless dress with Lacie's royal blue pigtail wig.

When I approached the bar, Cynthia's eyes popped open, and she stepped back. Then she hugged me. "Why do you look like an anime character?"

That confirmed the need for a picture. I scanned the bar for a willing photographer. Tristan stood by the front door with his hands in his pockets. With no one in line, and no IDs to check, I asked him to take my picture. I stumbled on the way to grab my phone.

"Whoa. Are you okay?" He grabbed my elbow to steady me.

"I'm feeling a little fainty vomity." No, vomity wasn't a word. But it got the point across.

"What do you need?" His eyes filled with concern.

"To sit down."

Tristan, ever the gentleman, assisted me to the nearby couch.

I sat down and focused on my breathing. In for four, out for four. I could do this. I stood up, got my balance, strode into the show area and sat with friends by the stage—all the while telling myself, *sit, relax, enjoy the show. You'll feel better.*

Done, done, and done. But I did not feel better.

Cynthia saw me after the show and immediately ordered me a ride home.

Thanks again for that. Knowing I had a twenty-minute wait, I ambled my way to the couch and flopped down.

My dear friend Kyle sat down next to me and held my hand. I rarely saw him outside of FIVE and always enjoyed spending time in his space. He wouldn't leave my side until my ride arrived. Then he helped me into the car.

The whole way home, I closed my eyes and focused on breathing. *Just get home and crash. You just need to make it home.*

I did make it home. But crash? Nope. Only if you count a near crash into the toilet after I ran into the bathroom to throw up.

After I finished, I steadied myself on all fours to clean up my own vomit. The joys of being single. Next, I hosted a small pity party for myself. I'd earned it, and I didn't have enough energy to do more. Overnight, I enjoyed a lovely rotation of vomit and diarrhea.

The next morning, KG woke me up with our daily call. We talked long enough for me to give her the full scoop. Afterward, I dropped the phone next to me on the bed and fell back asleep for most of the day.

The next day, I tried to eat, but my body betrayed me once again. I couldn't even keep down Pedialyte. KG, bless her heart, sent me groceries online. I hoped I could eat them eventually.

By day three, I panicked. Dehydrated and exhausted, I called my clinic. I begged them to give me fluids. I remembered them doing that for me one time. They agreed and set an appointment that afternoon.

I wanted to feel better—100%—I also might've had an ulterior motive to recover quickly. I had a plane to catch. I refused to even consider rescheduling the New York trip.

My care team balked at my decision. Even Adam called me and said, "I'm not sure you should go."

I listened to his concerns and promised him I'd be careful. I'd be gentle to my body.

First step, I asked for a ride to the airport. My wonderful colleague Shannon and her wife Bethany happily accepted my request. After we hugged goodbye at the curb, I slowly plodded to the ticket counter. I swallowed my pride and asked for wheelchair assistance. I couldn't remember the last time I'd sat in a wheelchair.

Minutes later, a young woman named Kylie appeared with an empty wheelchair. I told her about my cancer journey, and she shared an Emily Dickinson poem with me. It went something like this: *There's something benevolent in a sky full of stars. It takes a lot of darkness to see the stars, and out of the darkest times we see the most beauty.*

I tried to find the exact poem. I searched every combination of the words I'd heard. I gave up. If you find it, dear reader, please feel free to share the title.

As Kylie and I approached my gate, we were talking about my hair. Or lack thereof.

A woman sitting on the other end of the gate area piped up, "A while back, I decided to chop off all my hair. It was so liberating."

Excuse me? Did I invite you into this conversation?

Bless her heart, I believed she had the best of intentions. But in my humble opinion, there was a world of difference between deciding to get a fresh new cut and cutting off your hair because large clumps came out in the shower. I kept that last thought to myself though. I kept all of my thoughts to myself.

After two connections, I landed in LaGuardia. I still felt rough and accepted wheelchair assistance to the bus area. The kind gentleman who pushed me took me right in front of the Metro card machine. Fantastic. I only needed to get to Jen's place. A twenty-minute bus ride? Totally doable. Except that I didn't have a Metro card to refill. I'd thought I could get one there. Wrong. I awkwardly shifted in the wheelchair to scan each machine for a new card option.

After a minute or two, my wheelchair driver said, "One second." He crossed in front of me to one of the machines, then turned and handed me a Metro card.

"Thank you so much." I quickly looked in my wallet. I had exactly one dollar left from my last drag show at FIVE. "Please, have this." It was literally the least I could do.

I boarded the bus and slowly sat down. *Deep breaths. You're almost there.* I looked out the window as we crossed the Triborough Bridge and watched my favorite place come into view. New York City. Center of the universe. Well done if you caught the *Rent* reference. I stepped off the bus at 125th and Lexington and into a wave of relief. I still had cancer. I still needed to stop every few steps. But my soul felt better.

After a solid rest at Jen's, I agreed to take the subway together. We had important business to attend to at *Beacon's Closet*. She'd recommended the massive thrift store years earlier, but I hadn't visited yet.

We arrived at a line halfway down the block. I mean, I appreciated the COVID safety and letting a limited number of people in the store, but I could barely stand. I found a ledge on the edge of the building and sat, closing my eyes. I found out later that Jen snapped a picture at that very moment. I looked so peaceful. Who knew I was barely holding it together?

Within minutes inside, Jen found the most fabulous little black dress and magenta heels for me. I refused to buy them without trying them on first. I stood in yet another line and lost my will to wait. I sat in a window alcove and rested and let others pass me in line. For some reason, I felt the need to overshare. "Cancer is a bitch, amiright?"

"It is. I'm so sorry," one of the kind women replied.

Jen and I both tried on fantastic outfits. I stood next to her as she paid. She looked me over. "Let's take a car back."

Brilliant choice, my friend. That night, I relished her Saturday night tradition of family movie night at home. I barely moved from the oversized chaise in the corner of the room. After the movie, Jen set up my mattress on the living room floor, and I fell asleep just minutes after her three-year-old daughter Glory.

I woke up the next morning and rolled over gingerly to see the sun streaming into the room. It felt easier.

Before long, Glory asked to venture out for donuts. How could I say no? I washed my face with cold water and felt a rush of adrenaline. I held the railing tightly on the way downstairs, just to be safe. I had more energy, but still took my time behind Jen and Glory on the sidewalk. At one point, I stopped and took a deep breath. One thought ran through my brain. This was where I belonged.

After we procured the donuts, we went back to Jen's, and Glory and I sat together at the mini picnic table. We feasted on chocolate glazed and took selfies together. With each passing minute, I felt more like myself. I hovered around 85%. Not quite 100, but I'd take it.

I cautiously navigated the stairs and perched on the edge of a kitchen chair while Glory played diner, where she was owner/host/server/chef. Three-year-olds were fun. Before long, she found my burgundy ombre wig. I popped it on her head, listened to her squeal with glee, and quickly snapped a picture. For what it's worth, don't let a sassy toddler borrow your wig, she'll show you up in it.

After the excitement waned, I prepared for a thrilling afternoon with Jen. Drag brunch at LIPS. Heather and I had gone there almost three years earlier at Jen's enthusiastic recommendation. Heather and I had met at a mutual friend's party almost a decade earlier and had been friends ever since. Feeling energetic, I insisted on taking the subway. I stepped into LIPS and felt the same rush of excitement from 2018. The chandelier, the gold ceiling . . . it truly was a drag palace.

Jen gave her name to the hostess, and we were escorted to a table just off the corner of the stage.

I grinned like the Cheshire Cat. "This table, though!"

Jen shrugged nonchalantly. "I just told them my friend was coming into town."

I looked at the menu and realized it was a Broadway brunch. Could this get any better? Very well, I'll have the *Evan Hansen Eggs Your Way*! While we waited for our food, I asked Jen for a picture together. I felt better than I had in a week, and I'd cleaned up nicely. I checked to make sure I liked it and noticed a selfie I'd taken in the airport Friday. Both pictures gave me the perfect opportunity to embrace the meme: *how it started, how it's going*. I liked where I was going.

I enjoyed brunch to the fullest and sang along to every show tune I knew. My cheeks hurt from smiling. Near the end of the show, Ginger Snap, the host, performed a ballad. I did not see that coming. When I heard the lyrics, "I am brave, I am bruised. I am who I'm meant to be," my eyes welled with tears. I looked up to keep them from leaking out. The song built to, "This is me," and Ginger Snap ripped off her wig and tossed it into the air. It landed on a gold mannequin. I broke and cried my eyes out.

The next morning, Jen accompanied me to the bus stop on her way to work. We stopped at the corner of 125th and Madison for one last hug. I crossed Lexington and 125th without makeup, a wig, or a head wrap, and a stranger looked at me and said, "You're beautiful." Taken aback, I smiled and told her, "You're beautiful!"

And you, treasured reader, you're beautiful too.

Chapter Ten

MEMORIES

B Y EARLY OCTOBER, I fell into a bit of a routine. Chemo on Friday. Lay low Saturday and Sunday. Nurse my upset stomach for a few days at the beginning of the week. Feel better by the end of the week. I felt more energetic too.

One morning, I took my bike Winnie out of the garage and strapped on my helmet. I turned on my headset because KG's call could come any minute. I might not have many more days left to bike before the temperature dropped below fifty. Yes, many in Madison biked in the snow. I wasn't one of those people.

Sure enough, I felt my headset buzz two minutes later. I pressed the accept call button. "Hiiiii. I'm out with Winnie."

"Whyyyyy?"

"Because today is a chemo day, and I feel good right now, and I might feel like crap for days and days from now."

I got home, made breakfast, and took my usual one-song shower. I hoofed it to the hospital for my echocardiogram. Afterward, I went outside to catch my ride to treatment. My dear friend AB, also a sister breast cancer survivor, told me time and again to let people love me. Meaning, accept help. Guess I'd finally decided to listen.

I sat through my usual blood draw at the clinic and waited for Dr. Milliken.

He burst in with a twinkle in his eyes. "It's time to change up your meds."

"It is?" My 2018 treatment had been scripted from my first meeting with Dr. Milliken. He'd never wavered from that plan. This time around, chemo felt more like hacking my way through the Wild West.

"We're going to drop Taxotere. We'll keep Herceptin. We need to be careful about your heart."

Right, right. Many chemo drugs killed the cancer . . . along with other major organs. Important organs I might need later. Minor detail. "Of course."

"Your hair might come back. And maybe you'll even be able to taste things in time for Thanksgiving."

I remembered that from 2019. Herceptin fell into the category of monoclonal antibody, not chemotherapy drug. I beamed at him. I felt like I won the lottery. What a day.

Two steps inside my chemo room, I stopped short. So short the nurse almost bumped into me. She'd hung up streamers and a sign that read, *Happy Birthday.* But my birthday was still four days away. "Ya'll, I am winning this day!" I exclaimed to anyone who'd listen. Once again, the nurses at 1 South Park Street went above and beyond.

I raced home with enough time to change for my first book event. I glanced at my packed suitcase and thanked myself for being a planner. Yes, the event was across town at Bos Meadery. My friend Benjamin and their band Kat and the Hurricane hosted a monthly variety show there and had invited me to do a reading. I felt honored to be included. Did I really need a suitcase? Well, I had to pack copies of my book and table decorations.

I grabbed my *Cheers, Queers!* mug to hold pens. Venellope Von Schweetz and YAAS figures rounded out the decorations. I popped on my silver fringe flapper dress, bubblegum pink wig, and tiara. Thanks again for outfitting me, Dana. I'd "met" Dana online through a mutual friend during the pandemic. It had taken months for us to meet in real life. Naturally, at a drag show at FIVE. Blessed with more friends than I deserved, I waited for Heather to pick me up. I remembered when she'd driven me to my mastectomy surgery four years earlier and insisted on rolling my suitcase to her car.

We arrived and set up my table quickly. I watched a couple bands and drag performers as I waited my turn. I heard my name and felt butterflies in my stomach. But I strode to the microphone like I'd done it a million times. I looked at the audience, grateful for a few friends smiling back at me. I read the first chapter and prayed they couldn't see me trembling.

The crowd applauded. Dee Dee, the emcee for that night, turned her microphone back on. "Let's all give it up for Jaimie!" I'd bonded with Dee Dee back in 2018, months after my mastectomy, when she'd performed in my first benefit drag show. I felt the nerves fall away and smiled widely.

"Now it's time for a little Q&A. I believe this first question is from Susan." Susan regularly attended my brunches and had created the flier for my second drag show benefit. "When is the next brunch?" Dee Dee read.

I laughed and leaned into the mike. "You tell me, Susan."

"Who is your favorite drag queen in Madison?"

Nice try, Susan. An impossible question. I loved so many performers in Madison. I couldn't imagine choosing a favorite. No, ma'am, that was a question I refused to answer. I skipped back to my seat. Phew. I had survived my first book event.

Heather drove me home, and I quickly crashed. The next day, I barely moved from the couch. I had written REST! on my calendar. Yes, in shouty capital letters. If

I'd left it blank, I'd have planned things and been busy all day. I knew myself too well.

I woke up at 12:30 the next afternoon. I hadn't slept that late since college. I needed all the sleep. And energy. Tonight was my book launch at FIVE, an event years in the making. And how could I not have it there when I'd basically written a love letter to that community? I slipped on my gown. To be more accurate, I slithered into Kayos' gown. Our relationship had blossomed a few years ago back when we were backup dancers for a drag show pageant.

I navigated small piles of sand in the parking lot from fall volleyball. I squeezed inside the front door. Transported back in time, I remembered my first time there. The club had been so quiet that day, like you could hear a pin drop. Granted it was closed, and we'd only been allowed inside to practice for the pageant.

Tonight, only a few people sat at the bar, and there was a sense of calm in the relative quiet. I silently paid gratitude to this space and sprinted—more like fast-walked—to the dressing room.

Kayos, my host for the evening, greeted me first. "Well hello, Miss Published Author!"

I quickly greeted Dee Dee, Amethyst, and Alice, the rest of the night's performers and pushed the door open to a giant buzz of electricity. I couldn't believe all the friends who'd shown up for me. Every few feet, I found another congratulatory hug.

The queens performed one number, and I read from my book while they changed for their second. After my reading, Kayos announced the 50/50 drawing to benefit The Trevor Project, a nonprofit that provides information and support to LGBTQ young people twenty-four hours a day, every day of the year. My friends stepped up for them and raised $150. Minutes later, my friend Craig handed me a wad of cash. "Here, this is to match the donation. I love The Trevor Project."

After the second round of performances, Kayos brought me on stage for questions from the audience. After I answered the last question, she took back the mic and held it in her perfectly manicured hand. "I need all performers on stage."

What? Why? We never discussed this.

At least ten drag queens joined us. Josh stood next to me and put his arm around my shoulders. Gratitude hit me like a tidal wave.

Still confused, I rolled with it, counting on Kayos having a plan.

She covered her eyes to block the stage lights, then pointed to the bar area just beyond the stage. "I see you back there, come get your ass on stage." When they gathered around us, she handed out cups. She quickly *click-clacked* behind the stage's curtain and returned with a bottle of champagne. She popped the cork and stepped down the line pouring some for each performer. "If you have a glass, lift it up. That's

all of you in the audience too. To Jaimie, Madison's
sweetheart and a goddam published author."

My heart swelled inside my chest. I felt like I'd had
a blanket of love draped over my shoulders. I raised
my "glass" to the audience, then to my friends on
either side of me. Four years ago, I knew none of
these people. I stood in disbelief that I got to call them
friends. Never mind the crowd there to celebrate a
book that I wrote. I could have floated out of FIVE that
night. But I had books to sign first.

A week later, a memory on social media dragged
me back in time. Six years earlier, I'd staffed Rock
'n' Roll Brooklyn Half Marathon for my full-time
job. My main job for that weekend? Cheering along
the course in Brooklyn's Prospect Park. The night
before the race, I'd dressed to the nines in a tight
purple dress—cleavage courtesy of my Va-Va-Voom
bra—and the sexiest strappy heels. I'd looked pretty
damn good.

When I'd met up with Jen, she'd crossed the street
and given me a big hug outside the door to the wine
bar. "Girl, look at YOU." She'd pulled it open, and
I'd teetered inside. Immediately directing me to the
leather couch in the corner of the room, she'd held
her phone in front of her face. "Okay, now pose."

I'd leaned back and stretched out my long legs like
a supermodel.

"Just. Like. That."

Back at the hotel, I'd forwarded the picture to my then husband. Current ex-husband, for a variety of reasons, and heard him salivating through the phone. He'd told me he needed it printed poster size. I mean, could I blame him?

Fast forward back to 2021. I'd celebrated my forty-fifth birthday three days earlier. I missed my wine-bar-couch body. I didn't miss wearing a bra every day, but I missed having the curves to fill one. Time hadn't stolen them, cancer had. I needed to work through that with my soulmate. Why did he have to live over two hours away? I missed our impromptu frozen custard meetings. But we still had our phones. I forwarded Adam the picture Jen took.

Me: I don't want to get into it now, but I have a lot of feelings about this picture. Six years ago today.

Adam: Okay, I'm here when you want to talk.

In the morning, I was ready.

Me: I just miss that body, seeing it. I'm feeling bitter about it. I had the surgery to get rid of the cancer. I did it, and now here I am again. Like I did it for nothing.

Sidenote. I knew it wasn't for nothing. I'd made that choice to extend my life. To give myself a chance. And I'd had three years and countless fabulous memories because of it.

Okay, back to my soulmate's amazing words.

Adam: Yeah, I can see that. That's really hard.

Me: Thanks for letting me get that out.

Adam: I know this probably doesn't mean anything coming from me . . . because I don't like boobs . . . and am only slightly attracted to the female figure . . . but . . . you are beautiful and have a great body. And above that, you have a wonderful heart. I wouldn't change a single thing about you!

Me: <three loudly crying face emojis>

Was there ever a question why I called him my soulmate?

Chapter Eleven

HIGH HOLY DAYS

Two days later, KG's phone call woke me. I fumbled in the dark to turn on my headset, squinting at my screen. Lots of unread messages. What was the sense of urgency, people? Oh, right. My birthday. My friends had listened when I'd said the day was important to me.

I'd been celebrating all weekend. It was a Tuesday. So, I sat at my desk and worked. Around three thirty in the afternoon, my phone rang. I saw Adam's name and smiled into the phone. "Hiiiiiiii"

"Do you want to take a break from work?"

I had a flexible job working from home. Why not take a little break? I hadn't seen Adam in person since my last brunch in July. "Are you on your way here?"

"I'm already outside." He laughed.

"I'll be right down." I grabbed my keys and sprinted to the door.

We hugged, and I didn't want to let go.

"Should we do our third annual Café Hollander Birthday Dinner?" he asked.

"Absolutely."

"Or we could go somewhere else. Whatever you want."

"With a name like 'third annual Café Hollander Birthday Dinner,' I feel like we have to go there."

Adam and I talked and laughed that night like no time or distance had elapsed. He drove me home, and I read more birthday wishes. My heart swelled. I felt incredibly loved. At the same time, there was a pang. I remembered the final scene of *Sixteen Candles*. Yes, I'd seen that movie more times than I could count. I wanted to sit on the table across from someone with a big birthday cake between us. Even with all the friend love, I still felt drawn to romantic love.

No person in sight, I focused on my first love—Halloween. As much as I got into the holiday, I struggled to come up with a costume. With a few weeks to spare, I asked friends who or what should I be for Halloween. As much as I appreciated Nancy's "Awesome, as usual" quip, I needed something more concrete. Several friends suggested a unicorn, and I ran with it. I ordered the horn online while I figured out the rest. Thanks to Dana, I had the right wig.

A week before Halloween, I gave the wig a test run in public. I popped it on before chemo and patiently waited for my oncologist.

Dr. Milliken opened the door a crack and laughed. "Oh my God, amazing."

"Doesn't everyone roll into chemo like this?" I laughed and curtsied.

"Can we take a picture together?"

Happy to oblige, I took the selfie for us.

The next morning, I realized one costume wasn't enough. Sure, the official Halloween party was Saturday night at FIVE. But I knew people would be dressing up all weekend long. Like Halloween 2018, I wrestled with the decision of leaning into my almost bald head or not. I just didn't want to.

KG and I chatted about it, and she gave me the best idea. Regina George from *Mean Girls*, after she left the locker room.

Blonde wig? Check.

Short skirt? Check.

Bra? Check for dust.

Heels? Duh.

I only needed a tank top. After a lunchtime trip to two stores, I almost lost hope. But then St. Vinny's rolled in for the win.

I finished cutting two holes in my tank top and saw a new message from Soleil.

Soleil: Happy Halloween weekend! The all-revered holiday of gays everywhere <3 crying laughing emojis>

Me: Happy Halloween to you! I already have two costumes planned for this weekend.

Soleil: Omg yasss. I love it. FIVE Saturday and Sunday? I'm so jealous.

Me: FIVE all three nights.

Soleil: Omg yasssssss. Flirt with every viable person you come across <grinning face with sweat emoji>

Me: Best. Advice. Ever.

Soleil: It really is. Honestly, some of my best work.

I had a blast at FIVE that night and crashed quickly. After a restful day, I prepared to become a unicorn. The horn came with glitter. It did not include any kind of application directions, just a small container of glitter in pastel shades. How many queens had I watched block their eyebrows with a glue stick? I turned on my heel, marched to my son's room, and found an old glue stick. I smeared it across my cheekbones and patted the glitter on top of them. Success. I did the same on my nose, chin, and the outside corners of my eyes.

I strutted like a peacock into FIVE. I knew I'd nailed this costume.

Kayos confirmed it. "Miss Glitter Fantasy. I'm into it."

Later that night, I danced with my friend Haley and her wife Abbey. They were both so kind and generous to me when I'd separated from my ex-husband. We took pictures together, and I noticed my phone battery was low. I couldn't leave yet. I needed to be there for the costume contest. I turned my phone on ultra-power saving mode.

It turned out to be not ultra enough. I did manage to order an Uber that was twenty minutes away. I watched the clock and the door. Twenty minutes later, no driver. Then thirty. Then forty. It *was* Halloween weekend in a college town. Maybe I should cancel and try again? I only had 17 % battery. It wasn't going to last. I messaged the driver: *Please text me, my phone is dying.* Then turned ultra-power save back on and headed outside.

Fifteen minutes later, I turned off power-saving mode and had 0% battery. Not sure how my phone was still on. Either way, it seemed I was out of options. I returned inside, unsure what to do. I just wanted to go home and go to bed. I paced up and down the front area of the bar.

Dave, FIVE's owner, looked at me with concern. "Are you okay?"

"I was just waiting for an Uber, and my phone is dead."

"Do you want to charge your phone?"

"That would be amazing." I breathed a sigh of relief.

"Come on. Let's go to the office." When we got there, he handed me a charger cord, but it didn't fit my phone. "I'm sorry," he said.

As if he had anything to apologize for. I zigzagged back to my friends at the bar.

The bartender, Demetrius, asked, "Is this still you saying goodbye?"

Damn, he called me right out. But then again, he'd often witnessed my forty-five-minute farewells. "I'm waiting for my Uber and my phone is dead," I explained.

Oh, he mouthed.

"I'm trying to figure out who is the most likely to help me at this point." My laugh sounded tired. I saw Brandon out of the corner of my eye. Excellent choice. I retold my story to him.

He immediately offered to help. "I'll order you a car from my phone."

"Thank you so much."

"I got you."

He searched for options and found very long waits. What was this, New Year's Eve? I guess in Madison, Halloween might as well be that big of a holiday.

He picked the ride with the shortest wait.

I sat down next to him and set my phone on the bar. On a dim screen, I could see an alert. Two missed calls? You've got to be kidding me. Caller ID showed Uber. I ran to the front door with Brandon on my heels. I approached the car and opened the door.

"You must be Jaimie?" my driver asked.

I turned my head to Brandon.

"I'll cancel your ride on my end. Good night!"

I woke up ready to celebrate one more time. But I didn't have a costume. Well, not one I wanted to wear. In 2018, I'd personified Eleven from *Stranger Things*. I didn't think I'd ever wear that look again. I also didn't think I'd have this little hair again. But here we were. I felt sad as I pulled the light pink dress over my head. Was I right back where I'd been three years earlier? I thought for a second. Knowing I wasn't, I prepared to spend a third fabulous night celebrating my favorite holiday with wonderful friends.

High holy days indeed!

Chapter Twelve

ONLY YOU

T HE NEXT MORNING, I grinned as I remembered the weekend. But then I opened my personal email and swallowed hard. I saw *Jack R.* in the subject line, and my heart raced. My brain scrambled. I closed my eyes and saw him smiling on my patio. My palms went sweaty, and I clicked to my work inbox. I avoided opening that email for hours.

When I finally clicked on it, I saw I had more paperwork to complete. Four forms, to be exact, including Victim Rights Request, Restitution Request, Victim Impact Statement, and HIV/STD Testing Request. Had I not already done enough paperwork in the emergency room five months earlier? Did I want Jack to be tested for HIV/STDs? I had no idea. After a few minutes, I decided I did. I needed to know if I had cancer and an STD. I hesitated for a moment. I felt bad for Jack. For a nanosecond. Poor guy was going to be stuck and have his blood drawn. Wait, what the hell was I thinking? He deserved not one drop of my sympathy.

After I completed all the forms, I had another decision to make. Did I want to attend the hearings? Did I want to speak in court if my victim rights were discussed or decided? My head throbbed. I thought I'd finished the hardest part when I'd gone to the ER. Little did I know.

I turned on the radio as I considered a statement before a judge and jumped into a mindless task. I made my bed. The task itself took no mental energy. But it ended up being far from mindless. I pulled on the pillowcases slowly. They were still new. Five months earlier, the police had asked for my sheets and pillowcases. I cooperated and bought a new set. I hated the reason for the purchase. I set the pillow down, and my blood started to boil. Every single time I put my head down to sleep, Jack was in the room with me. Even if for just a moment. I sat on the edge of my bed. Inhale, exhale.

An all too familiar song came on the radio. I listened to "Only You" from the first season of *13 Reasons Why*. I let the music wash over me, and I wept. I cried for myself, for Hannah Baker, and for every rape victim.

Chapter Thirteen
CHOKING HAZARD

Pre-pandemic, Dee Dee and Anita built a following for their show at FIVE, *Choking Hazard*, which was simultaneously wildly unpredictable and blandly reliable. You never knew what was going to happen on the stage. My cheeks hurt from laughing so hard. I really missed them during the pandemic. When *Choking Hazard* made its triumphant return, the shows kept falling on the weekends I had my kids. That was a no can do. After a few months, Dee Dee posted the next show's flier. The stars aligned. I didn't have the kids. I commented: I CAN FINALLY MAKE IT AGAIN!!!!!

Julia was quick to make the deal even better. I'd met her by a rack of cool vintage clothes from her studio at my first book event with Kat and the Hurricane. She messaged me: Would you like to hire my limo service?

And by limo service, she meant a ride in her sweet minivan with heated seats. Gotta ride to FIVE in style, right?

We got there with enough time to wish my fun-loving, fabulous friend Marcos a happy birthday and meet up with Julia's friend Kay.

Mama Shaw invited all of us to join her table. She was Mama to so many at FIVE and biological mother to Demetrius. Front and center, per usual.

Dee Dee asked the audience, "Are you ready for your first performer?"

We cheered and screamed.

Susan squeezed alongside our table and set a paper plate at the front of the stage.

I wasn't sure what was on the plate, but I knew the first performer.

"Oh, Sheeza," Mama Shaw and I said at the same time.

Sure enough, Sheeza slinked onto the stage in full cat print leotard. And Sheeza's face? I might as well have been staring at a cat. Near the end of the number, Sheeza got down on all fours and ate off the plate.

"Is that cat food?" Mama Shaw asked me.

Knowing Sheeza, I figured it was.

At the end of the number, Dee Dee joined Sheeza on stage. Dee Dee answered the question without being asked. "You know that bitch just ate cat food. I saw them in the dressing room, watched them open a can of Fancy Feast. I told them they could have just used refried beans."

Sheeza stood by their decision. "No. That wouldn't be metal enough."

Halfway through the show, Dee Dee visited with the audience. "Who's here for their first *Choking Hazard?*"

Kay raised her hand.

Dee Dee crossed the stage and strolled to our table. "And who brought you here?"

"Julia." Kay pointed to my "limo" driver.

"Hey, Julia." Dee Dee winked at her. "And of course, Jaimie is here." Dee Dee extended her free hand in my direction. I felt like an exhibit in a museum. "Does everyone know Jaimie?"

Cheers and screaming. I'd never get used to that. Way to make a girl feel special.

Dee Dee pranced back to center stage to rejoin her cohost. "Jaimie wrote a book."

"Local celebrity," Anita chimed in.

"You can find it online." She paused and looked at me for confirmation.

I mouthed *yes*.

"She's also in a few local bookstores. She's a published freaking author!"

After the show, my phone dinged with a group message notification.

Kay ended up buying two books from me that night. Hmmm, I wondered when I needed to start giving Dee Dee a commission.

Chapter Fourteen

CRITERIA

I LOVED SO MUCH about my life and felt grateful for it all. And I wanted more. Contrary to my past beliefs, I knew I didn't need a romantic partner to be happy or whole. I could spend time by myself and feel content. But I did long for companionship. I hopped on dating apps when the timing worked for me rather than obsessively checking them. It seemed to work better that way for me.

One warm fall afternoon, I met Daniela in my neighborhood over lunch. Like I said, dating needed to work into my schedule. We talked easily, and I enjoyed that feeling. We said goodbye with a hug. About twenty minutes later, I saw a new message from her. Well, that was quick. Apparently, I'd made quite the impression on her.

Hi Jaimie. It was very nice to meet you. Thank you for taking time out of your day to meet with me. As said, I'm looking for the right connection with a person, male or female, and I'm not feeling that you and I would have the right chemistry to create magic. I full-heartedly wish you all the best. You are a strong woman, and it sounds like you have amazing support. Stay strong.

Okay then. I appreciated the up-front nature. But I wondered, did she have this form letter message saved and ready to go?

A couple weeks later, I connected with Margaret. On our first date, we met at a local coffee shop, talked until they closed, then took our drinks to the neighborhood sidewalks. Quintessential, right? I found her smart, interesting, and funny. She must have seen something in me because we went out again a week and a half later. We sat in a courtyard as the sun slowly set. She ordered an old fashioned. I ordered a Cosmo to honor the recent passing of Willie Garson. Rest in peace, Stanford Blatch. She understood the *Sex and the City* reference immediately.

I said goodbye and already looked forward to our next date. We texted often enough, but it was difficult to get another one on the calendar. That happened with two busy moms. No big deal. That lasted a week. On Friday night, we texted about how our week had been and made tentative plans for the following weekend. Just before noon on Sunday, I saw a new text from her. Excited, I couldn't help smiling.

Margaret: It looks like next Saturday isn't going to work for me. Just too much going on. I also wanted to be up-front and let you know I think I started dating a friend, and while it's obviously new and a little uncertain, I want to see where it goes, and I'm not great at juggling multiple dating prospects. But I like you and would be interested in staying in touch as friends if you're up for that. I totally understand if not.

Fine. At least I got an incredibly kind and thoughtful rejection. Still, I felt frustrated. I texted Adam. He had a way of talking sense into me.

Me: Why is dating so damn hard for me?

Adam: I'm sorry Jaimie. Dating is hard. And it seems especially hard for you right now.

Me: It really is. And other people seem to not have it so hard, which makes me feel even worse. Thanks for listening.

Adam: I think it's hard for most people until they find someone. You just haven't found your person yet.

Me: I guess that's true.

Adam: You're not going to settle. And I think a lot of other people settle.

Me: Where are they?! I don't want to settle, but I'm also tired of being alone. I get why people settle.

Adam: Yeah, it's hard, but they are out here somewhere.

Me: <three loudly crying face emojis>

I knew I texted him for a reason.

Days later, KG had exciting news to share. After wrapping ten years prior, *Dexter* was back. For us, it wasn't just a show. Eight years ago, I'd traveled to my first work event in Austin where KG had picked me up at the airport. She'd taken me to a local place for lunch. While we'd waited for our food, she'd mentioned *Dexter*. I couldn't think of a better topic to begin a crazy long-lasting friendship than a charming serial killer in cargo pants.

KG informed me today that the network offered a free 30-day trial and super cheap monthly subscription price promotion for this new season. "And the new *L word* is on there too."

Okay, I got it. She had me at *Dexter*.

As for *The L Word: Generation Q*, I needed convincing. I'd enjoyed the original, but a reboot? I wasn't too sure. I clicked on the show description and recognized a few returning cast members. Within minutes of the first episode, I prepared to binge watch the series.

At the beginning of the second season, Bette Porter oozed frustration on the romance front. She asked a question that stuck in my brain. *But really, what is the likelihood that I'm gonna be able to meet someone who meets all of my criteria and fits into my life as a mother?* Wow. Same. Writers, I'd be happy to pitch in and help with season four.

I hadn't written out my criteria. Not yet. If the person had children, we would have something important in common. But how important was it to have things in common? My ex-husband and I had a LOT of shared interests—and that marriage had imploded fantastically. Maybe it didn't matter.

Opposites attracted, right? Wrong. I knew I couldn't be with someone who contradicted me at every turn. If only I could find a happy medium.

The next week, I met my friend Laura at a fabulous bookstore/bar/coffee shop in town. Yes, you read that correctly. Several bookshelves sat on a brick red carpet just inside the front door. A section of low tables and chairs led to the most beautiful gray marble-topped bar I'd ever seen. I knew the manager Molly from when we were both enrolled in the Entrepreneurial Training Program. It was an intensive business-planning training program offered through the Small Business Development Center at the University of Wisconsin-Madison. Go Badgers!

Laura and I had connected on a dating app in the fall of 2020. After a fabulous brunch and traipse around the neighborhood, we realized romance was not in the cards for us and decided to stay in touch as friends. During our bookstore/bar/coffee visit, we caught up on each other's lives, chatting about work, future life plans, and romantic partners.

I had a vision of the two meshing for me. I explained it excitedly. "This is how it's going to happen. At one of my book events, I'll see her browsing books. She'll tell me she's here for the event. I'll coyly reply, 'Me too. I wrote the book.'"

I still hadn't written out my criteria for a partner, but I liked the sound of that daydream.

Chapter Fifteen

GRACE

W HY WAS I ALWAYS so unwilling to give myself grace?

As much as I loved my book event fantasy, I hadn't entirely given up on dating apps. I matched with River, and two days later we met at a local coffee shop. They simultaneously presented in both traditionally masculine and feminine ways. While I'd thought my next relationship would be with a woman, I told myself repeatedly that I was looking for a good human. As a pansexual, I felt an attraction to the person as an individual not based on their gender. A boxy suit jacket, plus earrings, and eyeliner. Minimal facial hair, which I appreciated. I enjoyed getting to know them and looked forward to a second date.

A few days later, River suggested a local brewpub. I quickly dolled myself up after an evening work call and braved the cold. I heard a fresh gust of air, and they appeared in the doorway. Immediately, I noticed a bit more facial hair than our first date. It caught me off guard. Our date was . . . fine. We chatted, but the conversation came to a grinding halt more than once. That rarely happened once when I was spending time with someone. By the end of the night, I just wasn't feeling it. I really wasn't sure what they were feeling.

When I got home, I hoped for no text. If neither of us texted and it just fizzled out, cool. But if they texted, what would I do? I couldn't even put my finger on why I didn't feel a spark. I slept poorly that night. The next day, hope stayed alive. Until just before two thirty in the afternoon.

River: How has your day been?

Me: Good. How about yours?

Well, good was overstating it. I was tired and nervous to hear from them. But was I really going to text that back?

River: Not too bad.

I didn't respond after that. Was that ghosting? Mayyyyybe. I hoped not, because I know how terrible that felt. But I also didn't feel like I had anything else to say in that moment. If River had texted again, I would have replied. A couple more bad nights of sleep, and I never heard from them again.

By Friday morning, I needed to talk about it with KG. "I don't know what it was. I just wasn't feeling it," I tried to explain.

"Okay," she started.

I mentioned the facial hair issue. "I kept thinking 'dude,' and I didn't want that." I stumbled around my thoughts.

"But if you're pansexual, that shouldn't matter."

Ouch. Way to hit me where it hurt. I understood pansexuality. I didn't understand myself. How could I still not know? How hadn't I figured things out by this point in my life?

But I didn't want to unload all that on her. She came from a place of love. "I know."

Over my lunch break, I tried to cure my frustration with a coffee shop visit. I justified the purchase with the few dollars that remained on my gift card. Inside, I stood behind the plastic partition behind the cash register and recognized my barista friend immediately. "Hi Alex, how are you?"

His eyes twinkled. I could only see his eyes above the mask covering most of his face. "Doing well. What can I get started for you?"

I glanced at the menu over his head and sighed. "Hot chocolate with peppermint syrup, please." RIP chai lattes. As much as I loved them, chemotherapy round two had killed the taste.

His head dropped before punching in the order. "Well then. Okay."

I shrugged and defended myself. "I know it's basic, but it's what I like."

"Hey, it's a classic. And tis the season," he rationalized.

"Exactly."

"Anything else for you, hon?"

"Nope that's it."

I sat down on the opposite side of the counter and caught up on notifications on my phone, not in any rush to get back to my work emails.

In the next several minutes, a number of people placed orders and left with drinks.

I stood up and headed to the pickup area.

"Mobile order?" another barista asked me.

I couldn't see a name tag, so I named him Caleb. Because he really reminded me of Caleb from *Thirteen Reasons Why.*

"No, but yesterday mine ended up with the mobile orders."

"What's your name?" Caleb asked.

"Jaimie."

Caleb grabbed a cup and handed it to me.

"Thanks, have a great day." I saluted him carefully with my cup and went to my car. I sat down and took a sip. Eww, coffee. I rolled my eyes at myself. About face. I know, lots of people would be thrilled to have a fancy coffee drink. But I wasn't most people.

Alex was helping someone else at the main register.

I waited my turn then asked, "Do you smell coffee in this? Am I losing my mind?"

He took off the cap, took a sniff, and confirmed, "Oh yeah, this definitely has some coffee in it."

"I thought so."

"I'm sorry. We'll make you a new drink."

"Thank you so much. I just don't like coffee. Yep."
I raised my hand. "The weird one at the coffee shop
who doesn't like coffee."

"It'll be right up for you."

I stood at the end of the counter this time. A
few minutes later, Caleb handed me another drink.
Apparently, I now had trust issues because I tried it as
soon as he left.

Coffee.

Again.

The label on the cup even said mocha. I dropped my
head and laughed. I didn't want to say anything, but I
also really wanted a cup of overpriced hot chocolate.
"I'm pretty sure this is a mocha." I handed the cup to
Caleb. "I ordered hot chocolate."

He looked at it. "Yep, it sure is. I'll make you a
new drink right away." He rushed around behind the
counter.

"Thank you soooooo much."

He handed it to me, and I felt like I could see a
smile underneath his mask. "Here you go, not a drop
of caffeine in the cup."

I laughed. "Perfect."

"Third time's the charm," he said with a sparkle in
his eyes.

"That's right. Have a great day." I smiled under my
mask and went outside.

I laughed at myself for spending that much time on a single cup of hot chocolate. Did I get irritated with anyone helping me? Not for a second. I gave them every grace. Life was so busy. How privileged was I to have the time to wait and the money to get this drink in the first place?

If only I could give myself that kind of grace.

Chapter Sixteen

COMPLIANCE

I SIGHED. I KNEW it had taken strength to even click on the link. But I still felt powerless. I left the meeting and my computer. My presence had mattered too. I'd complied for myself and for all the other women counting on me. This wasn't over. Not by a long shot.

Days later, Jack's name reappeared in my inbox. The court had scheduled the first hearing for the Sunday after Thanksgiving. Yes, the first hearing about my rape case. Eighteen months after the assault. I pulled up my sleeves to type, and my internal heater kicked on. I immediately emailed my therapist for an appointment.

A week later, I tiptoed around the topic during our telehealth session. I knew I needed to talk through it. I wanted her professional advice, but that didn't make it easy to bring up. I bit my lip and looked away from the camera.

"What are you worried about?" she asked.

I slowly turned back. "That he's going to say it was consensual. That I wanted this to happen." Tears stung my eyes. I couldn't look at her. "I don't know if I told you this before, but either I didn't remember it or I was ashamed. When we were sitting on my patio that night, we were talking, and I touched his leg." I looked up to see her reaction.

"That is not consent to have sex with you."

The finality in her voice didn't convince me. "I know. I just wish I'd been a stronger, more badass woman. That he had come on to me, and I'd said, 'Aww hell no,' and slapped him across the face." But I couldn't even piece the entire night together.

"You are strong. Coming forward is strong. You did the right thing. In that moment, you did nothing wrong."

"I know that. I just wish my case were stronger. I'm afraid he's going to get away with it completely and be free and clear to assault other women." The last thought made me sick to my stomach.

"I have to think he's worried."

"Maybe." I rubbed my temples with my index and middle fingers.

I understood the concept of consent. I had shared it with both my children from an early age in a developmentally appropriate way naturally. And still, once again, I struggled with giving myself grace. I needed reminders.

My therapist asked me to write those reminders on notecards after our call.

I grabbed three index cards and wrote one sentence on each card.

I did not give you consent.

You assaulted me.

You raped me.

I repeated them often over the next week.

Four days before the hearing, I reconnected with Kate. During our years of raising children, we rarely spent one-on-one time together. That weekend, we made up for lost time. We enjoyed a one-night staycation at a hotel on the lake in Madison. We strolled around museums together. We went out for a dinner "date" at a romantic restaurant. Time with her soothed my soul. And for the record, Kate is straight and happily married.

Late Sunday afternoon, a calendar reminder—*Prep Case*—jolted me back to reality. But what was there to prep? What was there to say, other than I wanted to keep Jack from raping another woman? As far as spending time and energy prepping, hadn't I given him enough of my time and mental energy already?

Delete. There went the reminder.

I decided to go to a drag show at FIVE. I could stew in my thoughts here or have fun with my friends there. Option B, please. I thought about what to wear. While no one would judge me if I did, I did not show up to FIVE in sweatpants. I'd been wearing a lot of black.

A fantastic color year-round, really, especially in the early winter. But I wanted to mix it up. So, how about the exact opposite? A winter white vibe. I'd just scored a fabulous dress from Upshift, my favorite thrift shop. As I showered, I thought about the color white a lot. A symbol of purity. Or maybe that's just what I'd learned growing up. Traditionally, brides wore white. Virginity and all that.

Was I pure that night back in May of 2020? I believed so. I reminded myself that I did nothing wrong. I didn't even know what was happening. I finished my makeup and questioned whether I'd wear a wig or not. I wondered if this was how Moira Rose from *Schitt's Creek* felt while getting ready. I pulled the dirty blonde wig on first. It just looked wrong. I tried the ombre black and the burgundy. No and no.

I looked in the mirror. Dr. Milliken had predicted correctly. The Herceptin-only treatment regimen had allowed my hair to start growing back. I had less than an inch. For the first time in months, I saw my own hair on my head. I rubbed the peach fuzz to confirm it was there. I closed my eyes and soaked up that moment. For the first time in months, I felt a little more like myself. I decided to leave the wigs at home that night.

My finishing touch? Earrings. I looked at a row I rarely wore. Jewelry didn't cross my mind when I got ready, and earrings got lost in the wigs. This barely-a-pixie-cut hairstyle offered me a silver lining.

I could show off long, dangly earrings. I grabbed a pair of silver sparkly snowflakes. Why not complete the entire winter white theme?

I arrived at FIVE and shuffled inside. I hung my coat in the closet and found Jacob leaning against the bar. His eyes widened, and his jaw dropped. For multiple seconds. "You look amazing."

Was there really a better way to start a night out? I cheered for the performers and soaked up the love around me. Just before I left, I set my alarm for eight fifteen. I would show up to virtual court with a clean face and business professional top. Out of respect for the court, not Jack.

I frantically logged in at exactly eight thirty. My heart raced as I waited to get clicked in. Deep breaths. I expected to see the judge and Jack in the courtroom together. I had it all wrong. There were two full screens of people on the call. Who were they?

Before long, the judge started reading the cases. Ahhhhh, I understood. I scanned the screen for Jack. Not there. Maybe he didn't show? I clicked the next button to reveal more attendees. In the middle of that screen, I saw his face. It was so dark in the room that he was in a shadow. Just as well, I really didn't want to look at him anyway. But I did click over a few times when the judge said his name. Would he react? Maybe show remorse?

The lawyer for the state spoke first. "Even though he denied it, the injuries were significant."

I felt like someone had shut the sound off on my computer. I could see her speaking, but I didn't hear anything. My brain jumped into a running commentary. He'd denied it. As I expected. Did he not understand consent? Had someone never taught him? I almost felt pity for him. Almost. But not quite. Why was I questioning the situation? I did not give consent. He raped me. End of story.

He looked blankly at the screen.

The judge explained that his presence that day showed compliance and denied the bail bond request.

Chapter Seventeen

DELETE. ALL. APPS.

A T THE END OF November, Josh and Jacob came over for dinner. All three of us sat on my L-shaped couch afterward, and I complained about dating. "The apps don't work for me. All the searching, the swiping . . . it's like a part-time job. It takes a while just to match with someone, then you message back and forth and do the mental gymnastics to get a date on the calendar around work and kids. Maybe a few days later, I'm ghosted."

"That's no good." Josh leaned back against the cushion and crossed his arms.

"It's too much," I agreed. "I just want to see someone across the room, feel a spark, and go from there. If I meet someone, it's going to be in real life."

"That's it. We're going to Milwaukee and hitting up the lesbian bars."

Jacob leaned forward and raised an eyebrow. "We'll be your wingmen."

I turned to Josh, who had the most intense work schedule. "Alright, when?"

"December will be busy with the holidays. How about the first weekend in January?"

"Book it, and cook it." I smiled.

After Josh and Jacob left, I started a mantra in my head. "Delete. All. Apps. Delete. All. Apps . . ."

Funny, it reminded me of "Defeat. All. Cybugs." Thanks for the memories, *Wreck-It Ralph.*

Once again, I deleted all the dating apps from my phone.

Chapter Eighteen

VIBE

A FEW DAYS LATER, the bookstore/bar/coffee shop hosted a Meet the Author event in my honor. I showed up in my red sequin floor-length gown, silver suit jacket, and a shimmery mask. I wanted to give off a sparkly yet professional vibe. I greeted Molly at the door with a big hug.

I glanced around the room and fell in love with the space again. It had a special shimmer, and not because of the Christmas tree twinkling in the corner. The tables and bar were full. I couldn't hear conversations, but I felt a happy energy bouncing all over the room.

Molly congratulated me and asked me to sign a small stack of books. Was this really my life? Midway through the evening, I strode up to the bar. Well, as much as you can stride in a tight dress with a thigh-high slit. "Can you make me something nonalcoholic in a martini glass? I want to feel like I'm having a drink, but I'll be driving home soon."

"Absolutely," the bartender replied.

I hung out while he made drinks, zoning out.

"I love this vibe." Someone in a glittery mask joined me at the bar.

Pulled back to reality, I looked at them. Sequin top and velvet suit jacket. Leggings and the coolest boots. I dug everything about this look. I was glad they couldn't see me blush through my own mask. "Thank you, I love your vibe too."

"Here you go." The bartender set a martini glass in front of me. The deep red liquid paired with a wintry garnish looked like it belonged in a magazine.

I grabbed the glass, turned my head, and wished my new velvet-suit-jacket friend a great night. Flushed, I rushed off to the overstuffed floral couch in the corner and my friends.

I spent most of the night visiting with them. I spent approximately one minute sharing about myself and my book after Molly quieted down the room.

The night flew by. I closed my tab at the bar. Out of the corner of my eye, I saw my velvet-suit-jacket friend. I remembered the daydream that I'd shared with Laura the month before about meeting someone at one of my book events. I had to say something.

In a move totally unlike me, I carefully sidestepped next to them. Now that I was there, I didn't know what to say. How did people do this? I still can't remember what I said exactly. I think I landed on the vibe appreciation route again. Something along the lines of "loving your vibe, and I'd like to get to know you better." Somehow, I got a phone number with a Chicago area code and a name. Carly.

I floated away from the bar in disbelief.

Later that night, I hemmed and hawed about texting. Too soon? Was I what the kids called thirsty? So, what if I was? I wanted to say hello, so I did. And waited an excruciating thirty minutes for a reply. Maybe it was a fake number? Or a pity handout?

Then she finally replied.

Carly: Hey. It was nice to meet you.

Worked for me. I knew we couldn't make immediate plans anyway. I was going to Austin to see my best friend in two days.

Chapter Nineteen

BIG TEARS

O N FRIDAY, I BOARDED the plane after work and pulled open the book *Greedy*. Why not dig into bisexuality and gender identity at 35,000 feet? Around ten thirty that night, KG pulled up to the curb at the airport, Lil Nas X's *That's What I Want* blasting from her car speakers.

I hopped in and reached over to give her the biggest hug I could. Settling into my seat, I noticed two foam cups in the cup holders. She'd bought strawberry and chocolate shakes, not sure which tasted better to me. How sweet was that?

We talked, laughed, and sang all the way back to her house. We went to sleep shortly after, knowing her one- and four-year-old boys would be up early.

In the morning, we had breakfast as a family and went to visit Santa. My heart swelled with gratitude being able to be there for those memories. Later that afternoon, the boys napped, and I went into the office/guest room to grab a sweater.

My phone rang. And I saw Dr. Milliken's name on the screen.

I froze. A Saturday phone call? What kind of news would warrant that kind of call? Not the warm and fuzzy kind.

I waited less than ten seconds for that answer.

"I studied your bloodwork results, and your cancer markers are increasing again." For the first time in three years, he sounded almost . . . defeated.

I sunk onto the office chair. I needed more information. "What does that mean?"

"We need another scan to be sure. I'll tell ya, though, I'm concerned that things are going to look worse."

My heart sank. "Okay," I barely breathed into the phone.

"But there are many times that I think it's going to go one way, and it doesn't. I'm not at all sure. I'm just nudged that direction."

I nodded, as if he could see me. "I understand."

"Another thing to consider is a study. I want to be ready. It takes about a week to get things moving."

I sat up a little taller. Proactive perked me up. "That makes sense."

"If you choose to participate, you can't have chemo for four weeks prior. It's never clear how long studies are open. This one is and probably will be for a month. If the cancer is growing, which we do not know yet, my advice would be to consider it."

I blinked while his words circulated around my brain. "Thanks for giving me time to think about it."

"Of course. There's no obligation. Studies don't do anything for me financially or professionally. They're just an option. Let's get the scan on the calendar, and we'll go from there."

I leaned back in the chair. A sense of calm washed over me. I appreciated how clearly he laid everything out. One step at a time. "Okay, that sounds like a plan."

"On a totally different note," he chuckled, "I was in *Mystery to Me* the other day and saw your book."

I laughed. Way to lighten the mood, doc.

"It was so cool. I had no idea you were an author and so talented."

"I told you I wrote a book." I smiled as I spoke.

He chuckled again. "Yes, you did. I'll see you soon. Take care."

"Sounds good. You too." I set my phone on the desk. The seriousness of the call crept back into my brain. I took three deep breaths before heading back downstairs.

From her spot on the couch, KG asked, "What was that about?"

My mouth dry, I swallowed hard. "I don't want to get into it right now. Can I have a hug?"

She stood quickly and met me in the middle of the living room. "Of course." She squeezed the tears right out of my eyes.

After I calmed down, I explained Dr. Milliken's call. We reassured each other that we'd sit tight and wait for the scan.

The next few days soothed my soul in the most special way. I drove with her to take her elder to preschool. I visited with her parents when we picked both boys after the workday. After dinner and some relaxing time, Yay Yay—KG's sibling and my wonderful friend—came over to join the fun. We all danced in the living room together and made salt dough ornaments.

Wednesday, KG drove me to the airport in the middle of the day. We sang and talked, but it felt different from the Friday night before. I wanted even more time with my best friend.

On the flight home, I worked through Glennon Doyle's *Get Untamed* journal. Feel it all, use it all. Hmmm, I was quite the expert at feeling it all. Why not lean into it? One page asked, *What moves you to tears?* In the last ten minutes, or can you be more specific? I decided focusing on what brought me to tears wasn't enough. I cry a lot, remember? So, I started a list titled "BIG TEARS." Which meant, what had me sobbing? Gasping for breath? Wheezing as the faucets turned on in my eyes?

First I wrote, *Tick, Tick . . . Boom!* Two weeks earlier, my sister-in-law Suzanne—my brother Cory's wife—had texted me: If you haven't already watched *Tick Tick Boom* on Netflix you must!!!

I knew I'd probably enjoy it, but I had to finish the second season of *The L Word: Generation Q.*

Sidenote: with all those cliffhangers, there better be a Season 3. I'd convinced KG to watch it during my visit and bawled through most of the movie.

Next I wrote, *Talk with Dr. Milliken.* What if my cancer really had spread? A glutton for punishment, I listened to the *Rent* soundtrack again. A support group sang, "Because reason says, I should have died three years ago." I gasped and couldn't catch my breath. Tears streamed down my face. Or should I say, BIG TEARS?

During my layover, I found a busy restaurant for dinner. As I perused the menu, I sang along with the nineties pop playlist. It gave me life. I didn't care if anyone could hear. Turned out, another person didn't mind either.

"Well, you have a beautiful voice," the man at the table next to me exclaimed. "You sound better than her!"

I stopped belting *Waiting For Tonight* momentarily.

"I could NEVER sound better than J-Lo, but thank you. She's an icon." I turned back to my plate and sang every song I knew in between bites. In my peripheral vision, I saw my neighbor pay his bill.

He stood up and approached my table. "Excuse me, can I ask you something?"

Oh boy. This should be interesting. I weakly smiled. "Sure, go for it."

"I just want to ask . . . I might be crazy. You can tell me to stop," he stammered.

In my head, there was a three-eye-roll emoji. "No, you can ask," I encouraged him.

"Do you have cancer?"

Here we are. "Yep, I do. Well, I did. And now I do again."

"I knew it," he shouted. "I mean, I saw your port." He gathered his bag.

I gathered a few more fries in my mouth.

He stood up and made direct eye contact with me. He lowered his voice, "My wife's sister had breast cancer. She had a transplant, and she's alive fifteen years later."

"That's amazing. I'm so glad to hear that." And I was.

"You're gonna beat it. I know you are." His eyes welled up with tears.

I didn't know what to say, so I said nothing.

"These are genuine." He wiped his eyes.

"Oh, I believe they are."

"I'm just so proud of you. You tell your most significant other, you made a man cry tonight."

Ummm, okay. Should I be proud of myself for that? Had I unlocked a special life goal? I gave him credit for not assuming husband or boyfriend and called it a win.

"A lot of people think they know what you're going through. I *know* what you're going through." He placed his hand on his chest for emphasis.

Did he? Did he know what it was like to be a woman without breasts? I believed his heart was in the right place, so I let it go.

How much time did I really have, though? Sure, any of us could be hit by a bus on any given Tuesday. But the thought of living like it's our last on earth? Trash. If I knew for sure I had one year left, I would make vastly different choices than if I was guaranteed another thirty.

I shed a few more BIG TEARS for good measure.

Chapter Twenty

NOBLE

FOUR DAYS BEFORE CHRISTMAS, I woke up before the sun and tiptoed to the hall closet. The second day of winter break, I wanted the kids to sleep as late as possible. I also wanted to keep my nervousness to myself.

I slipped on my boots and plodded to the hospital for my CT scan—at least it wasn't painful—then came home and dove into work. I only needed to wait two more days to meet with Dr. Milliken about the results.

The next day thwarted that plan. After lunch, an email notification rang like a loud bell in my brain. Subject line: MyChart Test Results.

I had a decision to make. Open the results, which I might not understand, or wait anxiously through one more day?

Curiosity killed the damn cat.

I carried my laptop into my bedroom and looked at the lab results chart first. My CEA number—my carcinoembryonic antigen, if you're into medical jargon—was the lab that showed the amount of cancer in my blood. And it was 249.1. Which meant nothing to me until I studied the past results. It had climbed since November and surpassed the amount from June 2021, before I'd started treatment again. The rest of the report read:

Multiple new liver lesions seen throughout the liver, the majority of which are measuring less than a centimeter in size. Whether these represent reactive change to treatment or progression of disease cannot be determined on this single exam. Recommend close interval follow-up. Increased sclerosis of the L5 vertebral body metastasis. Again, whether this is reactive to treatment or disease progression is difficult to tell on a single exam and close interval follow-up is recommended.

I imagined hearing the message from a robot. Your. Cancer. Is. Worse. <picture robot dance here>

My eyes stung, the tear ducts readying for some serious work. I sat as silent as a mime and let the tears slide down my cheeks. I refused to let my kids hear me cry three days before Christmas. I imagined them going to my ex-in-laws' house for the holidays and telling them my cancer was rapidly growing without me there to answer questions. Absolutely not. I thought about telling other friends—Jess, Kate, Betsy, or Jenni. I knew they'd be loving and supportive. I also knew they'd follow up with the million-dollar question: *Now what?* Since I didn't know, I held back.

But I had a few people I could tell. I sent the exact same message to KG, Liz, and Adam.

Me: I got my test results and curiosity got me. Want the update or want to wait until tomorrow (when I talk to Dr. Milliken)?

KG: Want it <two grinning squinting face emojis>

I copied and pasted directly from my chart.

KG: Ughhh.

Well said, my friend. Well said.

I gave the kids their Christmas presents the next morning. I wouldn't see them again until after the holiday, and it was a welcome distraction before my appointment.

Later that afternoon, I waited in an exam room for Dr. Milliken with a notebook so I could remember everything he said.

He walked in slowly and sat down across from me in a chair. "We have the results from your scan."

I swallowed hard. "I know. I saw the message, and I looked. But now I want to hear it in your words."

He pursed his lips, then exhaled. "I think the cancer isn't being held down by the treatment we're doing."

A little numb, I silently scribbled in my notebook.

"There are new spots in the liver. None of them are big, but there are many. One good thing is that I don't see spots elsewhere. There's a three-millimeter spot on your lungs. It's unlikely to be cancer. The spot on your L5 looks like scar tissue."

Okay, that was better than I'd expected. "Is this because we switched from the harsher chemo?"

He folded his hands and pressed them against his chin. "Short answer, it could be. We could go back to the Taxotere. But the cancer will figure out a way around that too. I think it's better to switch to an entirely different treatment plan."

Grrrrr. Why did the cancer have to be so smart? I knew he was right. "Okay." I listened and wrote.

"The way I see it, you have four options. One, you can switch back to the Taxotere along with pertuzamab and Herceptin. Which I think is the least likely to work. Two, you can participate in a study using CEA-targeted chemo. I'll get you more specifics about this if you're considering it." He rested his elbows on his chair and his hands on his thighs.

My phone rang.

I look down to see my older teen's face on the caller ID. "Do you mind if I answer this?"

Dr. Milliken waved his hand at me approvingly. "Of course, go ahead."

Bless his heart. I guess, with being a father of seven, he got it. "Hello!" I quickly answer.

"Hi Mom! Are you home yet?"

"No, I'm talking with Dr. Milliken—"

"Okay, I can go."

"Wait, what's up?" I asked.

"I wanted to get a book from the library, and I can't find my card. I wanted to borrow yours."

I dropped my forehead into my free hand. I'd asked. "Yeah, that's fine. I'll see you later. Love you, bye." I hung up.

Dr. Milliken chuckled and quickly composed himself just as his phone rang. "This might be the researcher." He flipped his phone over to look at the screen. "It's my daughter."

"Sure. Answer." As if he needed my permission. "Hi Dad. Do you know where the hair-cutting scissors are?"

I wasn't trying to eavesdrop, really. She just spoke really loudly.

He looked at me and shook his head slightly, one weary parent to another. "Downstairs by the workbench."

"I looked by the work bench. I didn't see them . . . found them!"

I stifled my laughter best I could.

"Not exactly an emergency." He sighed.

I didn't say anything, but kids, amiright? And back to the possible treatment plan. Minor detail of the day.

"So," he said, "I'm not sure that CEA-targeted chemo study I mentioned is the best option for you. A third option is to do -T-DM. It also goes by Kadcyla. It's FDA approved and the standard for women with HER2+ cancer. The fourth option is a study pairing T-DM1 and Palbociclib. It's been a great tool for women with HER2+ cancer. So, I'm hopeful that they can work well together for you." He sat back in his chair, maybe to give me a breather, then asked, "What are you thinking?"

What *was* I thinking? The options whirred around inside my head like he'd turned on a blender. I shut it off and thought about each of his ideas. I shot down the first immediately. He basically guaranteed that it wouldn't work. I supported research. Without ever putting on a lab coat, I could potentially help scientists cure cancer. I could help save others' lives down the road. "With all that we've talked about, I feel like the TDM1 and Palbociclib study is the way to go."

He scribbled on a notepad on his desk. "Let's start the process then."

"I mean, if I'm going to have cancer and I can be part of helping others down the road, why wouldn't I do that?" I shared my thoughts.

"It's very noble of you to think of someone else in this decision."

"Yeah, it's what I do." I smirked. Needless to say, I wasn't happy to have cancer. When I considered that my journey could help others, I felt a sense of peace and calm.

He swiftly set his pen down. "Will this help advance science? Of course. But I'm thinking of what might work best for you, and I think this study is it."

Very well then. Let's push science along and save my life.

Chapter Twenty-One

CURIOUS

I'D STARTED A NEW Christmas Eve tradition in 2019. It had felt odd to be single during the holidays for the first time in my adult life. The kids had celebrated with their dad, and my friend Karizma had encouraged me to come to FIVE. I'd had a blast talking, singing, and dancing the night away with friends excited for 2020. Little did I know. On Christmas Eve 2020, I'd stopped by FIVE long enough to pick up a to-go drink and had left with a FIVE gift card from Magali and fresh tamales from Max's mom. I could always count on Max for blunt advice, hilarious one-liners, and loving friendship.

Vaccinated and boosted, I dressed for Christmas Eve 2021. I slipped on my best silver sequin skirt—okay, my only silver sequin skirt—and a holiday sweater. I wasn't sure who would be out that night, but I had a feeling at least a few friends needed to end their Christmas Eve there.

I breezed through the back bar, and Marcos yelled from across the room, "Ahhhhhhh, Jaimie! I can't. This look is EVERYTHING."

I gave him the biggest squeeze, stepped away, and batted my eyelashes. "Oh, this old thing?"

Marcos and I caught up on life. We toasted to our fabulous friendship. After a while, I asked one of my favorite questions when at a bar with dear friends. "Can I leave everything here while I go to the bathroom?" By everything, I meant my wallet, phone, and ring. What? I didn't like it getting wet while I washed my hands.

On the way, I heard Ariana Grande's *Dangerous Woman* through the speakers. I had to sing along. Involuntary reaction. In the stall next to me, I heard someone else singing. Fun. Still belting it out, I made my way to the sink. If I hadn't been singing, my jaw would have dropped open. She had long dark blonde hair, bangs, and an amazing smile.

"I love your whole look," she said.

"I love yours too. I'm Jaimie."

"I'm Mary."

"Have a great night." I left and returned to Marcos and did my best to not stare at her after she came out of the bathroom.

Demetrius noticed as he made me a drink.

I swear, nothing got past him. I glanced Mary's way. "What do you think? Gay or straight?"

"Oh straight. Definitely straight," he responded immediately.

"Offfffff course she is," I replied with an eye roll.

"She's here with her gay bestie. She's straight." He handed me my drink.

"Yeah, I heard you the first two times." I seemed to have a knack for being attracted to straight women and gay men. Yay for me.

A while later, I zig-zagged through the bar to visit my friend Kyle. I told him about my crush and bobbed my head toward her.

He grinned and shouted, "Go get her, Girl!"

I rolled my eyes, silently thanked the DJ for the loud music, and sauntered back to the bar.

"Hey again." She stood next to me.

"Hey," I replied.

"This is my friend, Alex." She pointed to the guy next to her. "We dance together."

"Hi, nice to meet you," I said.

"We met." He clipped back. "Kayos introduced us."

Excuse me while I crawl behind the bar in embarrassment. I felt bad for not remembering. Then it clicked. He and Kayos were playing pool together the night I met him. "Yes! Hi. Nice to see you again."

The three of us visited for a while, then danced together. I went home happy for the new connection.

Two nights later, my friend Dana picked me up for the MadCity Drag Revue. I couldn't believe it was the last one for 2021. She treated me to a cocktail, and we sat down together. The performers were on fire that night. They put together stunning looks and gave so much energy during their numbers. Dana and I screamed and clapped for everyone. Near the end of the first set, I realized I needed more dollar bills to tip the performers. I raced to the bar, not wanting to miss a second. On my way back to our table, I saw Alex standing next to a support beam between the bar and the dance floor. "Hi! Great to see you again." I hugged him.

He squeezed back, let go of me, and turned his head. "Hey, and look who came. Mary is back tonight."

"Hi, you couldn't stay away, huh?" I hugged her too. "I'm going to sit. I'll see you after the show."

The show ended, and it was time to socialize. On the way to the bar, I caught a glimpse of the parking lot. All the cars were covered in snow. I know. It's not shocking for there to be snow in Wisconsin in December. But we'd made it through Christmas weekend without one snowflake. And of course, I hadn't checked the forecast. It was cold. What else did I need to know?

Mary's face lit up. "Oh my God, I've never seen snow before!" She raced to the door.

Alex sashayed past me and looked over his shoulder. "She's from Northern California."

Kayos joined us. "I have to show you how to make a snowball."

Kayos, Alex, Mary, and I ran outside. Kayos bent down and grabbed a generous amount of snow while Alex took a video. Freezing, we headed back inside. I trailed just behind Kayos and whispered, "I'm really into her, but I have no idea if she's feeling anything for me."

"I got you," she replied.

I visited with other friends at the bar, and I could hear her getting Mary's life story. "Oh, so you're just starting this QUEER journey in your life."

A few minutes later, Mary and Alex were on the dance floor. I decided, why not join them? What did I have to lose at this point? I stood next to Kayos. "You are a dear friend and icon."

"I'm here for you," she replied.

"Sooooo . . . " I pointedly looked at Mary.

"I mean, it's a risk," Kayos answered. "She's twenty-two and bi-curious."

"Got it." Eh. I could work with that. Maybe? I mean, there was a thirty-two-year age gap between Sarah Paulson and Holland Taylor. Might as well have fun and dance. And that's exactly what I did.

After a few songs, Mary said, "Alex and I are headed to Sham."

The Shamrock Bar and Grill. I could do that. "Mind if I join?" I must've been feeling particularly bold, and I didn't have to work the next day.

Alex drove slowly in the snow, and I messaged Dana.

Me: Annnnd I'm headed to Sham with Mary and Alex <face palm emoji> <shrug emoji>

Dana: Oooo... Is Mary who you danced with the other night?

Me: Yes

Dana: Be careful, the weather is not kind for driving.

Me: Alex is driving, and I'll Uber home later.

Alex parked on the street, and we trudged up the block in the snow to Sham.

The three of us stood at the bar and chatted. Three young men passed us, and Mary snapped her head in their direction. "There he is," she whispered.

"Where?" Alex asked.

She tipped her head toward the trio. "The tall one. We made out here a week ago." She looked nervously from side to side.

"Ohhhh, okayyy." I acted cool about it. But I was anything but cool.

"He's thirty-four. My mom would be so mad at me."

Welp. That was my cue. I ordered a ride home immediately.

The next morning, Dana messaged me.

Dana: How was Sham?

Me: Fine. I'm more embarrassed than anything else. This guy came in who she'd made out with recently. <face palm emoji> At least she is cool and fun. You're sweet to ask.

Dana: Embarrassed was not the response I was expecting. What do you have to feel embarrassed about? You're on a journey of making connections. You walk through the world with an open heart that is ready and willing. Other people are on their own journey. Sometimes our journeys match up with others, sometimes they don't match up exactly how we would envision they would. There is nothing to be embarrassed about there. You are brave to be vulnerable.

Now I was curious. How did I end up with the most amazing friends ever?

Chapter Twenty-Two

SPACE

I STARTED THE NEW year jumping through hoops to join the research study. I signed stacks of forms. I raced to the hospital for extra blood draws. I scheduled an echocardiogram.

Days later, the researcher rejected me because my liver counts were too high. Hello, McFly? Anybody there? The cancer had spread to my liver. I thought everyone knew that already. What had the researcher expected? I rolled my eyes and dropped my head into my hands.

After a few annoyed hours, I reframed the situation. The scientists and researchers had rules to follow. They didn't dismiss me haphazardly. I understood the study's rigid requirements, and it was not meant to be. Dr. Milliken decided to treat me with Kadcyla. He'd treated many patients with it for years. My longtime friend Tiernnee, who called herself Cancer Slayer, had just completed her sixtieth infusion of it. So, it sounded like a solid plan.

The next day I sat on the couch mindlessly watching TV.

A text notification startled me.

Josh: Hey friend! Still interested in a MKE weekend, or should we lay low with Omicron?

Me: Hey friend! I want to, but maybe it's an awful idea. I'm boosted, but maybe that doesn't matter with Omicron? What are you thinking?

After a lot of back and forth and more COVID decision exhaustion, we decided not to go. We planned a long lunch that Saturday instead.

Three days later, the dating app sent an email. *It's a match! Someone matched with you. Click to find out who.*

Okay, you got me. This wasn't a random marketing email to lure me into opening the app and tempt me to check out who was out there. Someone I had matched with earlier liked me back. If I was interested before, why wouldn't I be now? I added this one specific dating app back on my phone and went to my matches.

Merrill in a Wonder Woman costume. Stellar profile picture. I remembered swiping right. How could I resist?

We messaged for a couple days and set a date for Monday. We spent two and a half hours having cocktails and appetizers. We talked about her time in Italy, her dogs, and her nieces. I shared about my kids, my job, and musicals.

In two days, I was supposed to see the national touring musical of *Mean Girls*. I hadn't seen any theater in person for over two years. I couldn't wait.

Merrill went to the restroom, and I checked my phone. Dammit. Heather texted to let me know the show was rescheduled for the end of August. Oh well. At least my date was going well.

Merrill and I texted a bit over the next few weeks. First, she had a sore throat and didn't want to get together. Then she took a COVID test and needed to wait for the results. The following weekend, I had my teenagers. Phew. Dating during the pandemic was not for the faint of heart.

Never mind my pesky cancer journey. I drove to the clinic for blood work three weeks after my first round of Kadcyla. Cool. They tested my blood before every chemo treatment. Blood draw, doctor visit, chemotherapy. Like clockwork. Nothing new.

Until that day.

My CEA spiked again. It had doubled since the end of December. Not the trend we wanted to see. Dr. Milliken decided to hold off on treatment for one week. He wanted to be extra cautious. I could sit tight for seven days.

Two days later, Merrill and I scheduled another date for the following Friday night. That was one way to make the week go faster.

On Friday morning, I woke up with a different kind of energy. Chemo first, then date night. I kept things interesting, right?

Merrill and I met for Mexican. The place buzzed with energy, but our vibe felt flat. Question. Answer. Repeat. Don't get me wrong, I was all about learning through discussion, but I also needed a spark.

After an hour, I pushed for deeper conversation. "What are you looking for right now?"

"Honestly, I'm not sure." She tilted her head and shrugged.

"Oh, okay."

"I'm just not sure I really want someone in my life that much."

"Do you mean physically or emotionally?"

"I think both. When you're on your own for a while, you get used to things being a certain way. I like that space."

"Yeah, I get it." I did. And I didn't. I mean, why was she dating then? Guess it took a second look to figure out you didn't really want to.

We walked outside, hugged quickly, and said goodbye.

At least I enjoyed the guacamole.

Chapter Twenty-Three

THE BIG BAD

O N A FREEZING FEBRUARY Sunday night, I heard a notification and expected it to be her. Instead, I saw *Justine* on my screen, my oldest sister's name. She'd sent a group text to the entire family. My chest tightened. That couldn't be good.

Justine shared that she'd finally heard from the funeral home about Dillon. Her younger son had tragically died in a freak accident in March 2020. Because of COVID restrictions, the funeral home had paused all memorial services. Now, almost two years later, she could finally make plans. She'd arranged for a celebration of life in five weeks.

I bit the side of my lip. How could I make this work? I absolutely wanted to celebrate Dillon's life. And I hadn't seen my family in almost three years. Justine lived in Florida. I could not handle that drive by myself. I quickly searched flights. Nope, not in the budget. My brain hurt. My heart hurt. My eyes hurt.

I texted everyone back that I was still figuring things out.

Four days later, I drove to the clinic for my next Kadcyla infusion. We were back on track, right? Wrong. My CEA had skyrocketed like the price of gas in 2022. Yep, way too soon. The summer prior, my "high" number had been 232.9. At the end of 2022, there were five digits on the chart. CEA equaled 1,391.1. Once again, Dr. Milliken held off on treatment and ordered a PET scan on Friday.

I needed to rethink this Florida trip. Over the weekend I searched flights, praying for a miraculous sale. No such luck. On Sunday afternoon, I thought about the little I had in savings. People saved for emergencies, right? Or the figurative rainy day. If a celebration of life for my nephew didn't count as a rainy day, what did? I shut my eyes tight for a few seconds, sucked in a breath of air, then opened them and bought tickets for me and the kids.

At seven forty-five Friday morning, I drove to my PET scan. I told myself, "It's just another test. Get it done, and let the doctors figure it out from there." I drove home afterward and plopped myself in front of the computer. I had work to do, and a fun weekend ahead of me. The day flew by, and I flopped on the couch happily. The doctor had ordered a quiet start to the weekend.

Saturday started slowly with a book and a mug of hot cocoa. That night, Kelly and I caught up over cocktails.

I woke up bloated on Sunday morning. Ugghh. I needed to drink more water and exercise. Even on the weekend. Especially on the weekend.

After lunch, I drove to Kate's to see her middle child's stage debut in *Oliver!* The show was fabulous, and she politely and sternly invited me to her house afterward. I quickly understood why she'd insisted on the visit as the smell of warm chocolate chip cookies wafted my way. It didn't help with the bloating, but they were delicious.

Two days later, I headed to the clinic to discuss the results from the PET scan.

Dr. Milliken lightly tapped on the door before he came into the exam room. He was wearing an expression of defeat I'd never seen before. "It's worse. Your liver looks worse."

"Okay," I softly muttered. Why did my body continue to betray me?

"The vascular flow in the liver is impaired."

I shifted uncomfortably in my chair. "Does that have anything to do with this bloating?"

"Yes, it absolutely does. We can set up an appointment to drain some of the fluid."

"That would be great, thank you."

"The liver can bounce back, but we gotta get that cancer under control." He squeezed his fist and shook it.

Uhh, yeah. So do that, please.

"I'd like to try Trastuzumab. It's a relative of pertuzumab."

Cool. A snippet of the cancer drug family tree. I'd never been on either, so I didn't know what to think. "If that's your best idea, let's do it."

"If we can get approval by Friday, we start *Friday.*" The intensity in his tone pierced the space between us. He meant business.

Far be it from me to stand in his way. "Sounds like a plan."

"I have hope that we can get this under control in maybe a month. But if we can't . . ." His two-second pause felt like an eternity. And then came the BIG BAD NEWS. "I'm worried about less life. Is your family prepared for what might happen next?"

"Definitely not." They were all under the impression that treatment was moving along nicely.

"I think you might want to—"

"Meet with a palliative care doctor. I know." He'd offered me the opportunity back in 2018. I'd declined. I didn't think I'd needed the extra support. Dr. Milliken had confidently presented my treatment plan. Other than some nausea and a couple blood transfusions, I'd tolerated it well and leaned on my amazing support network of friends and family. I'd also thought palliative care doctors only worked with terminal patients. Incorrect. Diagnosed with a serious illness? You could have access to palliative care.

Today, I decided I needed to expand my care team. I had entered uncharted territory. I had the most amazing friends. Yet, I couldn't lean on them for this entirely. "Okay."

Standing at the checkout desk in a fog, I set three appointments for the following week. Fluid draw on Monday. Lab work on Wednesday. Palliative care doctor right after.

Three days after the BIG BAD NEWS, I started the new round of chemotherapy. I felt even more bloated and uncomfortable. I minced no words about that when the nurses checked on me.

"You know you could get a fluid draw," nurse Michelle explained.

"I'm going on Monday."

She put both hands on her hips. "You could go today!"

"They're not going to fit me in this afternoon." It was already pushing two o'clock.

"Well, not in the clinic. But you can go to the ER."

"I have a work event tonight. There's no way I can go to the ER and get home in time."

"Listen, your work will be fine. They don't need you tonight."

"I know they don't." I needed to be there. The event wrapped the entirety of my fundraising campaign. Seven weeks of long hours culminated in one virtual night.

Defeated, Michelle shook her head, turned on her heel, and left the room.

I raced home, ate some dinner, and turned on my computer. I fixed my hair and makeup. I swung open my closet door and looked down at my belly. Crap. The event called for formal wear. Don't get me wrong, I had dresses in my closet. In April of 2020, when most of the world lived in sweatpants, a friend challenged me to dress up every Friday. I thought I'd play along with Formal Friday for a month or two. I'd just celebrated ninety-nine consecutive Formal Fridays. But I couldn't fit into any of those dresses now.

I grabbed my trusty stretchy silver sequin dress, pulled it over my head, and tugged it down. The dress barely grazed my thighs. The back hung wide open. Not a prayer of zipping it. I swiped some red lipstick across my lips and logged into the event. From the collarbone up, I met the fancy requirement. Phew. I'd made it.

The weekend flew by. On Monday, I waited for AB to pick me up for the fluid draw. Our light conversation in the car put me at ease. Once inside the hospital, she didn't leave my side. Yes, that included during the paracentesis.

I looked at my stomach after the procedure. The area looked a little deflated, like a mylar balloon at the end of a day-long party. I wanted a bigger difference, but I was grateful for any change, however slight.

The following morning, I rolled out of bed and plodded to the bathroom. Dammit. My stomach looked bigger than yesterday. I pulled on an oversized pajama top and moved on with my workday.

The next day, I sat through yet another blood draw. I waddled back to the waiting room and waited for the palliative care doctor. My brain raced. I hadn't prepared for the visit with Dr. Gardner. I had no idea what she was going to say to me.

Less than ten minutes later, she called me back to an exam room. She told me how sorry she was that I was going through this. She asked about my family, my work, and my current mental state. She wanted to know how I understood my current diagnosis.

I repeated Dr. Milliken's words "less life" to her. My brain felt mushy. I didn't know what else to say.

"Your liver is very sick." Dr. Gardner spoke calmly and clearly.

I rested my hands on my belly as if waiting for a baby inside to kick me. Yeah doc, I know. My liver is a mess. I picked up my notebook and wrote her words verbatim.

"The cancer is spreading very quickly through it. If that trajectory continues, you might have weeks or months to live."

I felt like a giant bully punched me square in the chest, then put a vise grip around my throat. I blinked slowly, and the room went dark. It seemed like an hour passed between us, but it might have only been fifteen seconds. "Oh." My brain had nothing else to give.

"It's a bit of a race against time. The new chemotherapy might work. But even if it does, it might not outpace the speed of the cancer growth." She moved her left hand up at a diagonal angle. Her right hand moved toward the left hand but stopped at a lower point.

"You're talking about liver failure, right?" I needed this explained to me in simpler terms.

"Yes. If the cancer keeps growing like it is now, your liver would stop working."

"And if a major organ stops working, you die. Got it." With that explanation out of the way, I moved into planning mode. "Okay, so what's next?"

"You need to tell your children."

Another punch to my chest. "How do I do that?"

"You can tell them what I told you. That your liver is very sick because of the cancer. Explain it to them in a way they will understand. They need to prepare for the possibility of having less time with you."

Like I needed another reminder. I hated the thought of this conversation with them. I also trusted that she was right. I doubted this was her first terminal diagnosis rodeo. "Okay, I get it."

Within the next few days, I had several tough conversations. I told different people, but the reactions were very similar. I used the words my care team had given me. The room, or other end of the phone, almost inevitably silenced. Sharp intakes of air were common too. Then rapid-fire questions. *What's the plan? How are you doing? What can I do?*

Chemo every three weeks. I'm doing the best I can, all things considered. What could they do? That one required serious brain power.

Miss Planner needed to course correct. I used to think months in advance. After the BIG BAD, I barely considered a week ahead.

One Day at a Time. Not just a sitcom anymore.

Chapter Twenty-Four

CONTROL

A ND I FELT MORE in control than I had in months.
That March, cancer overtook my life. At least,
it overran my mind and my calendar. Within days of
the BIG BAD, KG asked if she could visit. We'd talked
about seeing each other over the summer. But what if
that was too long to wait? I hated the thought of her
spending money on spontaneous travel, never mind
being gone from her family. She refused to take no
for an answer. The trip was booked by the middle of
March.

Eleven days after the BIG BAD, I met with staff from
hospice care. Not my favorite reason to set an alarm
on a Saturday morning. One thought repeatedly
raced through my head like a toddler sprinting back
and forth across the room. *How did I get to this point?*

I mentally time traveled to a cool spring day in 2011.
I'd just dropped the kids off at school when my mom
called. My brother Cory had been diagnosed with
large B cell lymphoma. I remember being so hopeful.

He'd receive treatment and live a long, happy life. By May of 2012, the cancer had progressed too far. It was time for hospice care.

As the two women from hospice sat on the couch across from me, I snapped back to attention. I needed to focus on the information. I learned about the services they provided and the various staff on their team. Near the end of the discussion, I realized I couldn't have my cake and eat it too. If I chose to receive any kind of treatment to prolong my life, I could not receive hospice. Ah, critical piece of the puzzle. Well, I planned on chemotherapy until Dr. Milliken suggested otherwise. So, no hospice for me. At least not that day.

The next seven days mushed together like applesauce. I continued to work full-time while my life hung in the balance on the daily. I chose to share the information with a very small circle of friends. Between my family and those friends, I felt no peace. Every time I looked at my phone, I saw notifications for calls and texts in the double digits. An inbox-zero kind of gal, they drove my anxiety through the roof. Don't get me wrong, please. I felt so loved and supported. I also dreaded looking at my phone. Yes, I could've turned off the sound. But I still wanted to be reachable for my kids and care team. I can hear you arguing with me—just set it up so you only hear from the people you need to hear from. Yeah, when my brain was overwhelmed, obvious things weren't obvious to me.

The people closest to me had one consistent request. Updates. Daily updates. How was I feeling? Did the doctor have anything new to say? Had the prognosis changed? I truly wished I had answers. For their sakes and mine. But I didn't. It really made no sense to anyone. I knew the current plan. Chemotherapy scheduled every three weeks, pending bloodwork. And each time I drove to the clinic, I prepared for three possible updates.

Best update: Bloodwork's good. Proceed with chemo.

Mediocre update: Something is off. Hold chemo for a week.

Worst update: Chemo isn't working. There's nothing else we can do for you.

Since my first cancer diagnosis in 2018, I'd shared openly on social media about my journey. I had Stage 2B Invasive Ductal Carcinoma that was both ER+ and HER2+.

In the spring of 2021, I divulged my metastatic cancer diagnosis. But now, the BIG BAD news overpowered me. If I posted, I knew I'd be flooded with love and support. I envisioned hundreds of messages.

As much as I wanted to be fully open, I saw myself sinking in quicksand. I felt myself spiraling out of control. I needed guidance. I spoke with my therapist about all these feelings. She empowered me by insisting it was my business—and only my business—to share my updated diagnosis. With anyone. She encouraged me repeatedly to focus on feeling every moment and soak each one up.

Two hours later, the kids and I went to the airport to fly to Florida for Dillon's memorial. I asked them to wait for me while I checked us all in. I shuffled slowly to the ticket counter and asked for wheelchair assistance. Between my bloated belly and jaundiced skin, I gave no explanation. I didn't have to.

Once we were all settled on the plane, I took out my brand-new notebook. I wanted to write. I needed pen-to-paper reminders from my therapist. Ever the list maker, I wrote a single word on the top of the notebook page. *Control.* Yes, I found that title ironic. Nonetheless, I believed I could change that. In case you're feeling out of control, maybe this list will help.

- Drink water

- I choose when I respond to messages (if I reply within three hours or three days, so be it)

- Listen to music

- Let myself cry

- Live with integrity (my terms)

- Feel my feelings (all of them)

- I choose what I share . . . and with whom

- Seek joy

Our plane landed at eleven that night. My friend Katie, who'd suggested I see the chiropractor early on, picked us up at the airport. And proceeded to drive us two hours to the vacation house my brother rented. Yes, you read that correctly. Thank you again, Katie. You're a saint.

We tiptoed into the rental house in the dark, and my sister-in-law Stacy quietly directed us where to sleep. I hit the pillow like a ton of bricks after setting my alarm for not enough hours.

The following morning, I greeted my sister-in-law, brother Damian, their three children, and my younger brother John. Then we all hustled in different directions to get ready. We had a few hours before Dillon's celebration of life.

As Damian drove to the theater where Dillon had performed, I stared out the window, my mind racing. What was going to happen at the celebration? Who was going to be there? Could I feel happy to see more of my family even though my heart hurt for everyone who loved Dillon?

I got out of the minivan and immediately saw my parents.

My mom gave me her usual simultaneous hug and kiss on the cheek, and my dad hugged me longer than usual.

I followed them inside the main lobby. There were so many adorable pictures of my nephew. How could he really be gone? Inside the theater, I found and hugged my three sisters. I sat next to Jill and waited for the official celebration to begin.

I learned a lot about my nephew that day, which hurt even more. I didn't realize he made music. I silently punished myself for not getting to know him better. Near the end, a few of his friends came up to the microphone and told stories about him. Selfishly, I thought about myself. Would people be celebrating me like this in the summer? I closed my eyes and allowed myself to entertain the possibility. I wept silently for my own mortality and for Dillon.

The next three days, I soaked up time with my family and the eighty-degree weather. I wouldn't be wearing flip-flops when I got home. I refused to set an alarm and slept in. I made an exception on the second to last night. Half the house planned to get up and watch the sunrise. I slowly rolled out of bed and into the van, zoning out on the drive to the beach. I walked in the sand. As the sun rose above the water, I wondered if this would be the last beach sunrise of my life. I stared at the bright orange sky, and tears rolled down my cheeks. I decided to be grateful I saw it now.

The following morning, we packed up the rental house and made the two-hour drive to the airport. I hugged my brother, sister-in-law, and their teenagers unsure when I would see them again. If I would see them again. I managed to stand in line inside long enough to check in and wait for a wheelchair.

I grabbed the armrests and lowered myself down carefully. I looked down toward my feet and sighed. My ankles had completely disappeared. I looked like I was eight months pregnant. My brain couldn't compute what I saw. At least when I'd grown a tiny human, it had taken months for my body to change. The entire flight and car ride home, I looked forward to a shower. Yes, I had showered while I was gone. But I liked the idea of the warm water washing travel exhaustion down the drain.

The shower did the trick. At first. I ran my fingers through my hair. I felt a familiar sensation and looked at my hand. A large clump of hair was wedged between my fingers. I wiped it off on the shower wall and let my chin drop to my chest. No. Not again. I let the water run over my back and sobbed. I knew it was only hair. I had been through this twice before. But I didn't want to go through it again. It had just started growing back a few months ago.

I turned off the water, snapped a picture of the shower wall, and sent it to my best friend.

Me: Ok. Not sure if you'll get what's going on, but we'll try.

KG: Oh no. Is that your hair?!

Me: Yes. I about had a complete breakdown in there.

KG: <4 loudly crying face emojis> Aww hell no. Can't you just have that win?!

The last two times, my hair had fallen out exactly ten days after starting treatment. I'd made it to day twenty this time and thought I was out of the hair loss woods. *Me:* EXACTLY. And I don't know what this means . . . is the chemo doing something? (Yay) Or I'm just going to lose my hair anyway as one more punch in the stomach? *KG:* Fair question.

We had time for that question and more. KG boarded her flight to me that afternoon. School night. We all stayed up to greet their Auntie KG. I raced to her when she arrived. Well, my version of race, which was a slow shuffle. I squeezed her tightly, emotionally exhausted and thrilled to see her at the same time. Already after eleven, we crashed quickly.

The next morning, Auntie KG and I did the school drop off and drove directly to the clinic. In between bloodwork and a nurse practitioner visit, I fought with my laptop to sign onto a call with my nonprofit's CEO. Beyond frustrated, I started laughing.

KG asked me to let her help.

I handed over the laptop and got into the call minutes later.

KG joined me for the visit with my nurse practitioner, Bailey. I talked about my constant discomfort with my abdomen and now my swollen ankles. Bailey advised me to wear compression socks.

By the time we sat down in the chemotherapy room, KG had a set in her Amazon cart.

I usually sat through chemo alone. I preferred it that way. I worked with less distractions than at home. Unless I visited with the amazing nurses. That day, KG got in on the party. I watched my best friend and my hilarious nurse Michelle chat. So yes, I'd qualify it as a party.

KG and I filled the next seven days. We'd never spent that much time together. Turned out, we needed it. We were each other's person. We rode a roller coaster together that week. We hosted brunch and went to shows at FIVE. We shopped for comfy pajamas, which became my everyday attire. She found me a lap desk for the couch, and we also met with the funeral home, an estate lawyer, and a life insurance agent. Whew. I drove to the bank and made her a co-signer. Good thing I never worried about her draining my accounts. As if it would have been more than a trickle anyway. We laughed, cried, and soaked up the time together.

Chapter Twenty-Five

SMALLER

As MUCH AS KG's visit took a tremendous weight off my shoulders, it did nothing to change my pregnant-not-pregnant belly. If I reconnected with a friend in person, I'd update them on my current situation. To protect my time and energy, I kept quiet otherwise. I wanted to keep a low profile. But how could I hide the fact that I looked like I was about to pop when I posted a Formal Friday picture every week?

I got creative. I highlighted jackets. I used props, which included a couple different tables. I felt like Kerry Washington when she filmed Season 3 of *Scandal*.

Halfway through April, my former manager asked if I was up for a visit. Nicole and I had worked on the same team for years before I reported to her. She absolutely counted as a friend first. Even though we saw each other on Zoom regularly throughout the pandemic, I hadn't seen her in person since 2019.

I said yes immediately. A date was set for the first weekend in May.

A few days later, Adam invited me to be his plus-one at a medical school friend's wedding. Unexpected time with my soulmate? Sign me up. Cocktail dress attire? Let me get back to you on that. The clothes in my closet barely fit. Well, maybe if I could find something with a lot of stretch. Sure enough, I had a little black dress that fit the bill.

While Adam drove to the wedding, I asked, "How many people are going to ask me when I'm due?"

He let out his signature laugh, one of my favorite sounds in the world. "No one is going to ask you that!"

I tilted my head toward my midsection. "They might. I need something ready. I'll tell them my due date is July 13th."

"Okay. We'll tell them my boyfriend broke up with me, things happened, and I got you pregnant."

I cackled. "Absolutely no one is going to believe that. I'll just stick with July."

Turned out, nobody asked.

A quick week and a half later, Nicole arrived on a Wednesday afternoon. Pretty fabulous way to break up the middle of the workday. We hugged, visited for a few minutes, and sat back down at our laptops. Work still needed to get done, right?

A few times over the next couple hours, Nicole told me she needed to go get something at my front door.

Had she ordered dinner early? Nope. I shrugged and answered another email.

Suddenly, her head snapped up from her phone. "Come to the front door with me."

"Okay." Why not?

My friend Maggie stood just inside the door. Maggie had worked on the same team with Nicole and I for years.

"Whaaaaaaaaaat? You're here!" I ran over and gave her a big hug. I let go to see Nicole documenting the moment on her phone.

Over the next two days, I smiled and laughed more than I had in a long time. The three of us explored downtown together. We co-worked the next day and looked forward to dinner with our former colleague Shannon and her wife Bethany. Between bites of tacos and sips of a margarita, I laughed until I cried the happiest tears.

Another two weeks flew by before my next chemotherapy appointment. While I visited with Bailey, I asked for advice. "Is it safe for me to exercise?" I didn't want to run a marathon. But I missed my daily constitutional. I lived by a bike path and hadn't used it in a year.

"Listen to your body. If you feel okay to move, then do that."

A weight dropped off my shoulders. "I feel like all I hear is how I should be resting all the time."

"You don't need to meet anyone's expectations for what a 'sick' person looks like."

Life. Had. Changed. I knew that. But at that moment, her words were revolutionary.

The next morning, I got on my bike and rode the lakeshore path. Thanks again, Bailey.

Over the next few weeks, I still had my rage moments. Every time I touched my hair, another tuft fell out. Add water, and large chunks slid down the drain. I didn't want to wear wigs again. Wigs equaled questions about my health I wasn't ready to answer. My solution? I stopped washing my hair. I bought a tiny spray bottle and lightly spritzed it in the morning. I willed what I had left to stay. It worked. Sort of.

For too long, I spent every day angry. I literally growled at people on the bike path if they cut me off. I simmered with irritation at everyone and everything. I needed to feel differently. I grasped at straws and opened my notebook again.

Gratitude

- Compression socks

- Ankles

- Food – lots of food tastes *good* to me

- The hair that's staying

- ABBA (why hadn't I listened to them for so long?)

- Catching up on TV shows

I focused on gratitude like my life depended on it. Maybe it did. I studied my calendar since March 8. Since that BIG BAD day, I'd celebrated my 100th consecutive Formal Friday in a gold gown with a full photo shoot downtown. Thank you Susan, my amazing friend and personal paparazzi. I watched my teenage perform in their first musical since the world shut down. I cheered and screamed YAAASSSS at multiple drag shows. I spent time with supportive friends who loved me for me. I stood in the warm sand and watched the sunrise over the beach in Florida. How could I not be grateful?

At the beginning of June, Dr. Milliken ordered another scan. The last scan had fallen just before the BIG BAD. I had absolutely no idea what to expect. Over the past four years, I often predicted the outcomes of tests. This time, I couldn't even make one guess.

The day after the scan, a familiar number appeared on my phone screen. I answered immediately.

"Hi Jaimie, it's Bailey. We have the results from your scan."

My son in the other room, I grabbed my notebook and a pen. "Hi. Can you give me a minute? I'm going to move to another spot." In case of a BIGGER BAD, I didn't want him to watch me lose it.

"Of course. I understand."

I sat uncomfortably at the bottom of the stairs, balancing my notebook on my lap. "Okay, I'm ready." I pushed all the air out of my lungs.

"The lesions are smaller."

I scribbled furiously. I blinked a few times. "Oh?"

"There's no change with the spot on your spine."

Well, that was good. That hadn't even been on my radar. I'd thought we'd taken care of that a long time ago.

"We're going to continue this treatment every three weeks."

"That works for me." If it ain't broke, as they say . . .

Chapter Twenty-Six

SECOND OR THIRD

I MADE TREATMENT WORK, and then some. I lived determined to be grateful for every shred of good. Near the end of June, I decided to check my personal emails over my lunch hour. The one titled *Hearing Notice* nearly jumped through the screen at me. My stomach lurched. My desire to know beat out my need to vomit.

This is to inform you that a Pre-Trial Conference is scheduled to occur on August 5, 2022, by order of Circuit Judge.

My brain pulled me back to that night on my patio. I pinched the bridge of my nose, ran my fingers down my face, and squeezed my chin.

If only that would wipe all of it away.

If you would like to confer with the prosecutor regarding this case, we are interested in speaking with you and hearing your input regarding potential outcomes.

Yes, I would very much like to give you my input. I closed my fists so tightly my fingernails dug into the pads of my hands. I closed my eyes for three seconds and revisited the email.

Please contact me by email or telephone as soon as possible to discuss your options for conferring and to ensure your input is considered prior to this court event. Sincerely, Sheree Victim Witness Case Manager

I replied immediately telling her I'd like to connect with the prosecutor. I couldn't muster the strength to make another phone call.

She let me know that she would be in touch closer to the case. Fair enough. The process moved forward once again. And I didn't mind waiting until August.

The rest of the summer seemed to pass by in the blink of an eye. I soaked up as much sun and fresh air as possible. I adored Madison in the summer, Saturday morning Farmers' Market around the Capitol Square, and almost daily bike rides to the lake. And I also worked. Minor detail.

On a typical Tuesday afternoon, I bounced between online meetings, my inbox and spreadsheets. I focused well working from home. Until I didn't.

The sound of my cellphone ringing usurped my attention. I glanced to the side quickly to see City of Madison. I didn't understand the reason for the call, but I answered it anyway.

"Hello, is this Jaimie Sherling?"

I gulped hard. "This is she."

"This is Sheree from the District Attorney's office."

I felt winded. Thoughts buzzed around my head like a swarm of mosquitos. I noticed the date on my computer screen. Right. It was August now.

Sheree asked if this was a good time to talk. I mean, was there ever a good time for this? I remembered why I came forward in the first place. I needed to see this through. I shook out my hands and grabbed my notebook. "Yes," I told her.

Sheree dove in, and I scribbled furiously. She explained the difference between second- and third-degree sexual assault. In that moment, I shut off the emotional valve in my brain. I simply wrote. In the state of Wisconsin, at least, a second-degree conviction meant he'd be on the sex offender registry for life. He would have to go for treatment. With a third-degree conviction, he'd be on the sex offender registry for fifteen years and fall off it.

Emotional valve revolted and turned back on. Fifteen years? That was a long time. But was it long enough? The two thoughts batted around my brain like a Ping-Pong ball in a championship match.

"It's rare to immediately accept a second-degree charge. It often goes to trial. Are you prepared to go to trial?"

The question boomed in my head. Yes, I was. Wait, did I really want to do that? He'd show up with his fancy lawyer and look all contrite. One shred of reasonable doubt, and he'd be free to live his life without any repercussions. "Can I think about it for a couple days?"

"Of course." Sheree's tone turned softer. "Can we talk on Friday?"

Not my favorite way to start a Friday, but I took it. I gratefully accepted the time to think. I snapped a picture of my notes and sent it to KG. She texted back.

KG: We'll dig into this in the morning.

I finally let out the breath I'd been holding. As much garbage as life seemed to throw at me, I had a best friend at my side with a trash bag.

I spent my night focusing on dinner and a rousing tennis match. No emotions to work through whatsoever.

The sun barely on the horizon, KG made her feelings abundantly clear during our daily phone call. "Second. I want him to pay for what he did to you."

Always my fiercest protector, I'd expected that answer. I agreed and shared my concerns.

"I hear you. It's a lot to decide. I support you whatever you decide."

Turned out, second was the winner.

When I contacted Sheree, she thanked me for letting her know. Life returned to normal.

For two whole weeks.

I dined on my balcony with the kids and heard my phone buzz from inside. Eh, I'd deal with that later. We finished eating, cleaned up, and I took my phone from the counter. I unlocked it to see my ex-husband's name flash across the screen. Not my kids' father, my second ex-husband. Our marriage had fallen apart during my first run-in with chemotherapy in 2018. I rolled my eyes and growled quietly. What did he want?

Him: Just a heads up. A private investigator contacted me.

I knew it. My blood boiled and moved from my toes to my brain. My head felt like Mt. Vesuvius.

Him: In regard to the Otter Tavern night. I verified your story and had your back 100%.

I relaxed for a second. That was kind of him.

Him: The PI claimed you were known for falsifying information. If you want to talk, I'm more than happy to discuss.

Come again? I was known for what exactly? Steaming, I pressed the call button.

"Hey." He sounded sad. "I'm so sorry you're going through this."

I chose not to be upset with him. I only wanted more information. "Thank you."

"They're trying to disprove your story."

Of course they were. Bolts of anger coursed through my body. Slimy. Disgusting.

"The PI asked if I'd ever witnessed you being blackout drunk. Absolutely not. If I'd ever witnessed you using drugs. Absolutely not."

I seethed at Jack's lawyer's tactics. I simultaneously felt deep gratitude for my ex's honesty.

"Someone told the PI that you're full of half-truths and lies. They're trying to paint the story that you're a liar, a drunk, and that you sleep around."

Maybe the PI had missed a calling to art school.

Chapter Twenty-Seven

NOT QUITE A BOW

IN A BLINK, I felt a familiar chill in the air, the sun set sooner, and I crunched across leaves as I walked around my neighborhood. While squirrels scurried around me preparing for winter, I prepared . . . to wait.

For the record, waiting wasn't really my thing. I didn't want to wait for the rape trial to be over. I didn't want to wait to find love. I didn't want to wait to get clear answers about my cancer. But I also didn't own a time-traveling DeLorean or a genie in a bottle or a crystal ball. So, sitting on the bottom step of an infinite staircase to the unknown became my one and only option.

If the rape case continued to move forward on schedule, emphasis on *if*, jury selection would start in February. That was almost three years after I was drugged and attacked. Yes, let me say that again. Three. Years. That's after I came forward within twenty-four hours. I'm not judging anyone for reporting three or ten or thirty years later. Or never sharing their story. Not for a single second. I did hate feeling naive. I'd allowed myself to believe that if I divulged sooner, justice would be served more quickly. I'd handed the police DNA on a platter, for crying out loud. Yet the system proceeded at a snail's pace. And justice? Wasn't guaranteed.

That brought us to love. As much as things changed, they also stayed the same. My inner circle remained the fiercest, most loving support network anyone could ask for . . . ever. But romantic love? That was a mystery even Scooby Doo and the gang couldn't solve for me.

My therapist and I spoke at length about it. Did I have a black-and-white expectation that I had to have a partner? Maybe a constant sense of urgency made it more difficult for me to live in the present? Had I created a pressure cooker of possibility and then stood in my own way to finding love? In case you're struggling with any of this, let me share my therapist's latest piece of advice—which was and wasn't what I wanted to hear. She told me to have hope. She said, "You might find someone. You just never know." And with that, she handed me a serious dose of reality. *I might not find someone.* As I aged, there could just be fewer possibilities for potential partners. I needed to make peace with that. But could I? I'd like to say yes. But it felt a little like Wile E. Coyote and the Road Runner signing a peace treaty.

And I couldn't forget about the cancer. My body wouldn't let me. In the early fall, my liver became my enemy. My belly ballooned back to BIG Bad days' size. On forty-degree days, I wore legwarmers that fell below my knee. But not to make a fashion statement. Anything around my waist—leggings, pants, tights—hurt too much. I wish I could say it got better after a few weeks, but around-the-clock pain became my new norm. I felt stretched like a rubber band, pulled within a breath of snapping. I bought new over-the-knee socks. It was only going to get colder. Days crawled by while the weeks flew by. I counted them in threes. I'd potentially have chemotherapy every three weeks and a scan every three months.

In March, I wrestled with the uncertainty of my existence on a daily basis. Would I live long enough to take first day of school pictures? Could I take my kids out for Halloween one more time? I hoped to be able to watch at least one of my children graduate from high school. The second one loomed too far in the distance.

Near the end of the summer, Jen gifted me a book with a caveat. She passed along *You Can Heal Your Life* and said, "I don't know if this will serve you. Just in case it might, it's yours."

To boil it way down, Louise Hay wrote that "your thoughts control your life." In case you're about to toss this book in the trash, please don't. You're so close to the end. Also, I can't say I agree with every word verbatim. I'm not posing that I thought myself into a cancer diagnosis. At least for the moment, I did not plan to stop chemotherapy. But thinking more positively, that was a solid life plan, right? And honestly, what did I have to lose at this point? Perhaps some affirmations would give me some peace. In case you're down for this, I'll share one of hers for fun. Here we go. Say it with me. *My mind is cleansed and free. I leave the past, and move into the new. All is well.*

I was down for believing all is well.

Turned out, I'd become more willing to learn too. If I do say so myself, I've made some breakthroughs. I refuse to take all the credit. I listened to wise sages who pointed me in the right direction and handed me a shovel and toothbrush. I dug deep, and discovered more about myself and navigating my life through some seriously bumpy terrain.

I hope you'll indulge me sharing. Wait, when did this become an inspirational self-help book? Eh, let's go with it.

I'd heard once or twice that I could be hard on myself. I've told myself things I would never say to a friend. During the weeks of pain level ten, I scolded myself often. I hated being so short and feeling so ready to snap at anyone and everyone. I couldn't stand not being able to think of words and put coherent sentences together. I understood it was the physical aches and lack of sleep. I didn't care.

Ann, a former life coach of mine, gave me an idea. She encouraged me to try something new. "I want you to put both hands on your heart. Breathe. Then, talk to yourself. In the kindest, most gentle way. Like you are your own dearest friend."

I scoffed a bit in that moment. Two weeks later, I relented. This is what I had to say:

It was a really hard week. And you did your absolute best. You listened to your body. You fed your body. You fed your children, which was no easy feat with one of them being a wildly tall teenage boy who eats you out of house and home. You helped another teenager celebrate their 18th birthday. You had some amazing interpersonal discussions about life, friendship, and navigating high school. You learned about a new treatment plan. You advocated for yourself. You asked questions. You asked the questions a second time and repeated them back because you're getting three hours of sleep a night. You allowed yourself joy. You soaked up a longtime favorite Halloween tradition with your kids. Thanks again, Downtown Madison Family Halloween! You did all that and paid attention to your limits. I bet all of that was extremely hard to do. I see that. I see you. You are strong. And I know you're tired. No, exhausted in your bones and fatigued from trying to stay strong.

So lean on people how and when you can. Keep accepting help. If the help will actually serve you. Why not use wheelchair assist after your paracentesis? When a friend reaches out to make plans, make the most of them if you can. A chill dinner can be restorative. Protect your heart. Keep listening to music. Belt along if you want. Yes, even while walking to the parking garage in your building. Or down the grocery store aisle. Brilliant choice making that Santana Lopez playlist. Glee *wouldn't have been the same without her. Do your best to maintain your sanity. Yes, that includes saying "serenity now" out loud while dropping the kids off at school. I see you taking care of yourself. Keep it up. You're doing great, Sweetie.*

So writing this second book? Turned out I had a lot to say. I wanted to wrap everything up in a bow at the end, but life isn't like that, no matter how much I wish it was. Life's messy and confusing and shocking. Sometimes all you can do is get out of bed and face each day.

And if you cry a lot along the way, I'd say you're in good company.

Acknowledgments

In a perfect world, I would thank every single person who helped this book become a reality. In my current sleep-deprived, chemo-brain state, I know I would forget someone. And that's unacceptable. I have the greatest people surrounding me, and I'm forever grateful for all of them. So, I'm sending love and appreciation to everyone who was a part of this in some way. You know who you are. Thank you!

About Author

Jaimie Sherling is a joy seeker, drag ambassador, and the founder/designer of YDY, Sweets—a clothing line created for her sister breast cancer survivors. Her first book *From Queens to QUEENS: How the Madison Drag Community Saved My Life* shared her journey through cancer, divorce, and creating a circle of true friends. She lives in Wisconsin with her two kids. When she's not working at her day job or trying on piles of clothes at thrift stores, you can find her screaming *YAASSSS* surrounded by a bunch of queens.

BEFORE YOU LEAVE

T HANK YOU FOR FINISHING THE BOOK
Before you go...

- Consider a **review** on Amazon.

- Share on your favorite social media.

- Buy a copy for your friends.

Reviews really are golden to writers. Please take a few minutes and **write one now.**

I'd love a personal note. Feel free to contact me at ydysweets.com or message me @jaimiesherling on Instagram

Made in United States
North Haven, CT
05 February 2023